LIGHTS IN THE FOREST

Rabbi Paul J. Citrin was ordained by the Hebrew Union College–Jewish Institute of Religion in 1973. The focus of his rabbinate has always been in congregational life. His passions are education, Israel and social justice. He is the author of a children's novel, *Joseph's Wardrobe (UAHC 1987), Gates of Repentance for Young People*_(co-authored with Judith Abrams, CCAR, 2002), and *Ten Sheaves* (Create Space 2014). He lives in Albuquerque, New Mexico, with his wife, Susan Morrison Citrin, and they have four children and eight grandchildren. He serves the Taos Jewish Center on a monthly basis.

LIGHTS IN THE FOREST

Rabbis Respond to Twelve Essential Jewish Questions

EDITED BY

Rabbi Paul Citrin

✦

CENTRAL CONFERENCE OF AMERICAN RABBIS

5774 NEW YORK 2014

Editorial Advisory Group

Library of Congress Cataloging-in-Publication Data

Lights in the forest : rabbis respond to twelve essential Jewish questions / edited by Rabbi Paul Citrin.
p. cm.
"This volume is a harvest and sharing of thirtynine rabbis . . . These rabbinic respondents were ordained between 1974 and 2013, thus giving us views from two generations"—ECIP introduction.
Includes bibliographical references and index.
ISBN 978-0-88123-2202 (pbk. alk. paper)
1. Reform Judaism I. Citrin, Paul J., editor.

BM197.L565 2014
296—dc23

2014018253

10 9 8 7 6 5 4 3 2 1

CCAR Press, 355 Lexington Avenue, New York, NY 10017
(212) 972-3636
www.ccarpress.org

Contents

When a person walks through a forest on a dark night, and meets up with another person who has a lantern, he no longer gropes and stumbles in the dark. But, at the crossroads they part, and the one without a light must again find his way in the darkness. If a person carries his own light, he need not be afraid of any darkness.

—Rabbi Israel of Rizhyn (d. 1850) (from Martin Buber,
Tales of the Hasidim: The Later Masters, 62)

Preface

Many Jews today wonder or even explicitly ask, "What is Jewish faith? What does it mean to me, in my life?" So too, those considering Judaism want to know about Jewish faith and how they could partake in it. The beginning of a wide variety of responses comes with understanding the meaning of the Hebrew word for faith, *emunah* (אֱמוּנָה). *Emunah* means confidence and trust. *Emunah* does not refer to blind belief, assent to reason-denying principles, or accepting bequeathed dogma.

A person of *emunah* has confidence that the universe is undergirded by a life-sustaining, unifying force that is the source of moral insight and ethical imperative. One who possesses *emunah*, according to Jewish understanding, trusts in the goodness of life and its blessings. That trust includes a radical conviction that salvation—repairing ourselves and human society—is an eternal summons and possibility that is built into the fabric of the cosmos.

Emunah flows from a searching heart, a heart of openness and yearning. At the same time, we enhance and strengthen *emunah* in our world by becoming, each one of us, persons who embody trust, confidence, loyalty, and integrity. *Emunah*, then, is more than a personal philosophy. It is a religious stance or attitude. It must, perforce, demonstrate its living reality and power in our interpersonal relations, our *tzedakah*, our compassionate deeds, our honest self-reflection.

We modern Jews are not the first in history to seek *emunah*, to struggle with its meaning and contents. Moses beseeched God, "Let me behold Your Presence" (Exodus 33:18). The Psalmist made his understanding, his bewilderment, and his hope manifest for all to read. The Rabbis of two millennia ago wrestled with questions of *emunah;* the result is a cornucopia of wisdom known as midrash. None of these searches for *emunah*, however, resulted in an organized theology or Jewish philosophical system.

By contrast, Philo of Alexandria (first century BCE), Saadyah ben Yosef Fayumi (tenth century CE, Babylonia), Y'hudah HaLevi (eleventh century CE, Spain), and Moses Maimonides (thirteenth century CE, Egypt) set out consciously to create systems of *emunah* for Jews who were influenced by and acculturated to alluring majority cultures whose views and values challenged Judaism. During the twentieth century, a number of Jewish thinkers responded to mass immigration from traditionalist Europe to an open, volunteerist, democratic American society. They also dealt with the meaning of the Shoah (the Holocaust) and the question of God's place in a world where the Holocaust and the bombing of Hiroshima are permitted to occur. In the first quarter of the twenty-first century, we Jews continue to be challenged in our quest for *emunah*.

The American social context today confronts Jewish values and ideals in several important respects. Radical individualism takes priority over community consciousness, support, and participation. Materialism and acquisitiveness trump compassion for individuals in need. Family relations and sacred celebrations take a back seat to time spent pursuing commercial or professional endeavors. Scientific discoveries in the realms of subatomic physics, neurobiology, and genetics prod us to examine and rethink our understanding of what it means to be human. A flurry of writing by the likes of Dawkins, Hawkings, Harris, and Hitchens—one-dimensional and superficial in their understanding of religion and particularly of Judaism—challenge us with an articulate atheism.

Jews today who would build *emunah* in their minds and hearts are frequently overwhelmed, and thus stymied, in the attempt to create meaning and values from the soil of Judaism. For some, it means taking an unresisting path of giving up a quest for *emunah* as personally irrelevant. For others, pursuing a spiritual philosophy and life path has led to Zen practice, Buddhism, Hinduism, Sikhism, or Christianity. It happens that some who have taken such paths away from Judaism find their way back to Jewish *emunah* after winding journeys through alien territories.

More than ever, contemporary Jews seek *emunah* to live. To develop personal *emunah* does not require an academic theology or a constructed philosophical system. It rather calls upon those who have struggled, read, thought, experienced, and searched to share with us and to guide us. Any sensitive, thoughtful person may be such a guide, but rabbis by dint of interest, study, and ongoing teaching are especially suited to help in the quest for *emunah*.

This volume is a harvest and sharing of thirty-nine rabbis who have labored to cultivate *emunah* in their lives and in the lives of the people they teach. Each rabbi has chosen to respond to questions under one of three categories: (1) On God, (2) On Our Humanity, (3) On the Jewish People. Thirteen rabbis have responded to each category in thoughtful, personal voices. Most of the rabbis serve in congregations. A small number are rabbis in academic arenas. These rabbinic respondents were ordained between 1974 and 2013, thus giving us views from two generations. The gender ratio among them is about even. (The reader can find brief biographies of our contributors at the back of this book.) It is, therefore, my hope to present readers and seekers with a spectrum of ideas and convictions that will stimulate or deepen personal pursuit of *emunah*.

Despite this book being an anthology of the thought of Reform rabbis, in no sense is it intended to be or to be viewed as an official Reform Jewish theology. The very notion of such is antithetical to

Reform Jewish *emunah*. The short essay answers you will read in this collection surely represent the thought and experience of the respondents, but they also reflect the influence of those who taught them, whether in the classroom, in their own reading of Jewish thinkers, or through the questions of congregants and students. While statements of *emunah* differ one from the other, the common feature among them is intelligent and intelligible presentation as well as passionate commitment to this teaching endeavor.

It has truly been a privilege and a learning opportunity to work with the thirty-nine colleagues who have contributed to this book. I thank them for their efforts especially because I know how many and great are the demands upon their time. I am most grateful to the Publisher and Director of the CCAR Press, Rabbi Hara Person, for her constant patience, insight, guidance, and encouragement. In addition, thanks go to Rabbi Steven A. Fox, CCAR Chief Executive; CCAR Press staff members Debbie Smilow, Ortal Bensky, and Cori Carl; Rabbi Adena Kemper and rabbinic intern Liz Piper-Goldberg; as well as Debra Hirsch Corman for copyediting, and Barbara Leff for the beautiful cover. My deep appreciation goes as well to the members of the editorial committee who reviewed this book and made helpful suggestions: Rabbis Linda Bertenthal, Ben David, Geoffrey Dennis, Stephen Fuchs, and Patricia Karlin-Neumann; and to the members of the CCAR Worship and Practice Committee, in particular Rabbis Elaine Zecher, Joseph Skloot, Beth Schwartz, and Rabbi/Cantor Alison Wissot.

The title of this book, *Lights in the Forest*, points to the rabbinic respondents as those who carry light, who guide those groping for answers, who lead them to further thought and study so that they may carry their own light of *emunah*. May the readers of *Lights in the Forest*, seekers of *emunah*, make their way with growing confidence and trust.

RABBI PAUL J. CITRIN, editor

Section One

ON GOD

1. What is your concept of God, and how has your view changed through your life?

2. What is God's relationship to suffering and evil?

3. What is the connection between God and ethical values?

4. In our science-oriented society, how do you speak of God's role in nature and in history?

RABBI KENNETH CHASEN

1

As a teenager, I couldn't make much sense of the God-images that had been most frequently presented to me as a child. The God I learned about in religious school was anthropomorphic and omnipotent, and I just didn't see God operating as an almighty human being in the world. A further complication was that I, like so many, had been hung up on the literal meanings of the Jewish prayers. As I grew into young adulthood and began applying my critical thinking skills to the siddur, I grew uncomfortable with the notion of a God who intercedes to grant healing, bestow abundance, and free captives. There were just too many worthy people praying for those blessings and others but not receiving them. I concluded that I couldn't believe in a God who would listen to the penitent yearnings of some while rejecting the desperation of others. If I was going to be a believer, I needed a concept in which I could believe.

I found that concept during my college years, when I began to study the writings of Rabbi Abraham Joshua Heschel. I can still recall the specific teaching that reintroduced God to me in a way that I could understand:

> When in doubt, we raise questions. When in wonder, we do not even know how to ask a question. . . . Under the running sea of

> our theories and scientific explanations lies the aboriginal abyss of radical amazement. Radical amazement has a wider scope than any other act of man. While any act of perception or cognition has as its object a selected segment of reality, radical amazement refers to all of reality; not only to what we see, but also to the very act of seeing as well as to our own selves, to the selves that see and are amazed at their ability to see. (Heschel, *Man Is Not Alone*, 13)

When I first discovered these words, I remember feeling as though they practically proved God's existence. Suddenly, I sensed a horizon of knowledge that was wondrously beyond my view and my control as a human being. God wasn't some non-corporeal Santa Claus, deliberating over human requests. God was where the unknowable was known, and in relation with that God, my job was—and still is—to demonstrate both humility and gratitude in the face of a bounty of blessings I can hope neither to produce nor explain.

2

A congregant of mine who is struggling with lung cancer recently approached me for some spiritual counsel. She asked, "Can you help me figure out what to pray for? It is more than I can bear to pray for my cancer to clear. I just can't stand having too much false hope and ending up so disappointed." I told her that I understand her hesitancy to pray for a miraculous healing. She would have to think about what would be left of her emotionally and spiritually if her prayer should appear to go unanswered. However, that certainly doesn't mean that I told her to refrain from praying. I believe that the exercise of prayer itself possesses the power to produce some significant measure of the strength she most needs to face an uncertain future. Her prayers can also intensify her focus on making a blessing of each day, of each minute of her life, reminding her that none of what she had previously assumed to be "normal" about living is, in fact, to be taken for granted, nor is it permanent.

This is how I look at God's place in the experience of suffering. I do not believe in a God who selects certain children to be inflicted with leukemia, so neither can I believe in a God who selects certain children to be cured of leukemia. It is no accident that the overwhelming majority of traditional Jewish prayers are expressions of gratitude, not requests for intercession in our lives or world. The religious discipline of Judaism inspires a person to sense blessing in things that humans too often consider ordinary or expected—our breath, our freedom, our abundance, the many wonders of the universe. The goal is to engender the question "Why me?" in moments of good fortune, not just at times of suffering. If God's worth is to be evaluated solely on the basis of whether our wishes are granted when we pray, there is no humility in prayer. We are not seeking God; we are seeking to *be* God.

We will, of course, always yearn for a world without evil or suffering. However, it is the very existence of curse that enables us to recognize and hunger for blessing—and it is the existence of curse that will forever fuel our efforts to unleash more and more of God's light through our own actions.

3

At the very end of his life, having survived the Nazi camp of Terezin, Rabbi Leo Baeck republished an article, entitled "Mystery and Commandment," that he had written before the war. Clearly, he felt that even in the aftermath of one of humanity's most striking displays of moral depravity—perhaps especially in its aftermath—his words regarding the interplay between theology and ethical behavior still rang true:

> And reverence is man's feeling that something higher confronts him; and whatever is higher is ethically superior and therefore

> makes demands and directs, speaks to man and requires his reply, his decision. It . . . can manifest itself in the other as well as in oneself. Reverence is thus the recognition of the holy, that which is infinitely and eternally commanding, that which man is to accept into his life and realize through his life—the great impelling force, the active aspect of wisdom. (Baeck, *Judaism and Christianity*, 172)

Baeck's words have long guided my own understanding of the fundamental role that God plays in the ethical strivings of humankind. When I try to look at life through the eyes of wonderment—with Heschel's concept of radical amazement as my inspiration—I marvel at the majesty of the human species, imbued with its profound capacity for and inclination toward moral reasoning and action. Remarkably, we are created in a manner that enables us to discern right from wrong and to feel the tug of our consciences toward right. In many instances, moral behavior can seem to collide with the kind of Darwinian self-interest that undergirds evolution theory. Sometimes, when we choose other-interest over self-interest, we make ourselves at least marginally more vulnerable to danger, insecurity, or loss. I believe this happens precisely because of that "feeling that something higher confronts" us—something that I name God—but something that seems to create a deeply powerful compulsion even for those who claim to reject a belief in God.

As Baeck indicated, we are commanded by that higher presence. It is inescapable. It demands a reply, over and over again throughout our lives. This is how we live out the covenant that resides at the very core of the Jewish tradition: "You shall be holy, for I, *Adonai* your God, am holy" (Leviticus 19:2).

4

I have long seen the science-versus-religion debate as something of a canard. They are not in competition with one another. They are not even attempting to answer the same set of questions. Science is the endeavor through which we attempt to answer all the questions of "How?": How do the planets function? How does the sun rise every morning? How do humans procreate? How do our brains function? Our scientific acumen leads us to an increasingly sophisticated understanding of "How?" Science, however, has never found—nor will it ever find or even seek—the answers to "Why?": Why are there planets? Why couldn't the laws of nature have been made to operate differently? Why am I inside my body, and you inside yours—at this precise time in human history? Why couldn't we have been created in a manner impervious to illness or injury, enabling us to live forever? "Why?" questions are the eternal questions, and no amount of research into "How?" will ever unlock the mysteries of "Why?" In my theology, the answers to "Why?" belong to God.

The impulse to see science and religion as being at odds with one another arises from our discomfort in coping with the vulnerability of human existence. We humans don't like acknowledging that we can't know "Why?" Our everyday lives are an exercise in the exertion of control over the world. We were created *b'tzelem Elohim* (בְּצֶלֶם אֱלֹהִים), "in the image of God" (Genesis 1:27), so that we could fill our non-Shabbat time as partners in Creation. This is what makes us feel secure and powerful. There can be no doubt that the expansion of our understanding of "How?" has enabled us to change the world and the course of history. However, it has also tricked us into believing in an illusion—that we might someday be capable of knowing everything. Admitting our frailty, our helplessness before that whole wealth of information that only God knows, that we want desperately to know, makes us feel small and vulnerable. This is particularly true when we are suffering because of our frailty. I have long believed that cultivating a religious sensibility—developing a discipline of gratitude for the countless blessings that elevate our lives and that exist squarely in the terrain of "Why?"—can provide tremendous comfort at those painful times when we are reminded that we cannot know "Why?"

RABBI MIKE COMINS

1

"If to believe in God means to be able to talk about him in the third person, then I do not believe in God. If to believe in him means to able to talk to him, then I believe in God" (Schlipp and Friedman, *Philosophy of Martin Buber*, 24). It was only after ordination, at age forty, that I internalized this teaching from Martin Buber. You don't *think* God; you *meet* God. You don't *reason* God; you *perceive* God. God is not in a concept; God is in a moment.

I feel most "spiritual" in the most "material" places, like in nature or in the bedroom, and closest to God when hiking, praying, conversing, creating art, making music, or practicing the Taoist moving meditation, qigong. But in my upbringing, abstract thinking about God replaced explicit instruction on how to meet God in the world and what that might look like.

When I think of a religion, I ask: Where is the spiritual action? For Buddhism, it is in the mind; for Christianity, in the afterlife. Jewish practice is well grounded in everyday life, but the spiritual action, I was taught—the divine target of Jewish prayer and ritual—was always in some intangible, non-physical dimension accessed through speculative (and to me, unbelievable) arguments and ideas. Despite a wealth of God-moments, for most of my life, I was a wannabe when it came to belief in God.

What changed? Buber, through I-Thou relation, and Rabbi Abraham Joshua Heschel, through awe and wonder, taught me that one gets to God not by taking a mental turn around the physical world, but by engaging with it as deeply as possible.

Rabbi Lawrence Kushner's works made Jewish mysticism plausible for me. When I was taught qigong, based on the same Chinese medicine that brings us acupuncture and other healing therapies, I immediately felt the energy called *chi*. I realized that a central claim of Jewish mysticism is true. *Chiyut* (חַיּוּת), a Chasidic term meaning "divine life-force," and derived from *chayim*, "life," flows through the world, and I can tap into it most anytime I try through deep listening, meditative awareness, and prayer. I embraced the *Zohar*'s description of God (through Kushner) as the River of Light.

Most important, I feel *chiyut* in my body. Once I paid attention to the *feel* of connecting to godliness, my body became a thermometer to measure and guide my Jewish practice. I have learned which activities and spiritual practices, readily and reliably, bring me into God's presence.

Even the most mystical, sublime, "spiritual" moment is experienced in a body. Would it not make more *sense*, and give people the realistic, achievable expectation of meeting God in the everyday fabric of their lives, if we acknowledge that we encounter God, and that we best gain knowledge of the Divine, not through abstract, unprovable speculation, but through the experience of our bodies in transcendent moments?

2

Heschel writes, "This is the most important experience in the life of every human being: something is asked of me. Every human being has had a moment in which he sensed a mysterious waiting in him. Meaning is found in responding to the demand, meaning is found in sensing the demand" (Heschel, *Who Is Man?*, 107–8).

As long as I can remember, I have felt the call to the right and the good. When Heschel explained this to me as a manifestation of the Divine, my intuition was validated.

An all-good, all-powerful God could not let drunk drivers kill innocents, let alone allow the Holocaust. When Harold Kushner suggested that God is not all-powerful (or chooses not to be all-powerful), my intuition was validated.

I do not believe God operates like a super event planner according to a master plan, or that God is an idea, or that God can be reduced to an interior psychological state. Rather, I know that *chiyut* is always running through me, in dialogue with the world. Just as the divine flow influences me, I influence it, through thought and action. When I pray for someone's healing, I don't believe that I'm petitioning a God who makes human-like decisions as to who will live and who will die. But I know how to build *chiyut*, the divine life-force, within me through meditation and movement, and I know how to send it toward other people through prayer, and I know that it has an effect.

✦ ✦ ✦

Life could not have evolved without the rotation of the earth and the motion of continents that create hurricanes, earthquakes, and tsunamis. Human acts of malice are optional, but disease and natural disasters are as necessary as the air we breathe. Since I don't believe God personally decides when and where disease hits, when my mother died of cancer before her time, I didn't ask, "Why her?"

All that sufficed until I experienced the long, slow, painful death of my father due to Lewy body dementia. Then I knew the anger of Job in the face of random, unbearable, undeserved suffering. I cried out in protest—to the God I don't believe in!

I am baffled and offended by the depths of human suffering and human evil in God's good world. Nothing alleviates or justifies the pain.

And nothing makes truth, justice, beauty, and love less noble and extraordinary.

Every day, I say thanks to God for the privilege of living in this marvelous world. When I can't, I stand with Aaron and Job before the mystery, in silence.

3

When an infant cries in your arms, what the child needs becomes your command. When my spouse suffers, what she needs is my response-ability. Buber located I-Thou moments of transcendence, in which we are in dialogue with the world around us from a posture of communion and empathy, as the source of ethics. This prompted Buber to understand that God is present in every moment of genuine dialogue.

For me, God's role in I-Thou is the hardest part of Buber's thought to fathom. Rabbi Eugene Borowitz helped me to understand. God permeates transcendent moments of I-Thou as an inexplicable but real sense of "quality" (Borowitz, *Renewing the Covenant*, 101). We feel the call mentioned above by Heschel. We are lured beyond self-interest and moral mediocrity.

I believe God's presence is real in ethical moments because I am not reasoning, projecting, or inventing this invitation/demand that I act my best. I am reacting to it. I-Thou doesn't reinforce my habits, assumptions, and predispositions; it shatters them. I am called, attracted, and pulled to the right and the good by meeting God's transcendent quality, an experience available to me every day.

Does recognizing God as the source of ethics in moments of transcendence make a difference in our lives? As practicing Jews, we are called to do *t'shuvah* (תְּשׁוּבָה), "repentance," particularly on Yom Kippur. Most of my life, I dutifully dwelt on my shame and guilt. I thought about self-change and didn't change much. Now the transcendent, right-brain God-moments of a fruitful Jewish, spiritual practice draw me out of my neurotic thoughts and show me what is possible. I am pulled forward, by light and hope.

4

Based on Enlightenment philosophy, modern thinkers compartmentalized science and religion into neat cubicles—science reveals facts; religion generates meaning. Postmodernism emerged as this and similar value/fact dichotomies were proved false.

Science cannot explain everything, and during the previous century it constantly overreached, especially in the social sciences. But when it deals with what it can competently explain, no source of truth is more certain, not to mention more noble, effective, and fruitful, than scientific method.

Truth is not optional for the spiritual seeker. We cannot base Jewish belief and practice on wishful thinking. Maimonides's great philosophical work *Guide for the Perplexed* explicitly integrated the science of the time, neo-Aristotelian thought, with Judaism. It never would have occurred to him, or any other Jewish thinker of note, to ignore or deny the best knowledge available. Otherwise, Judaism becomes distorted or, worse, trivial. We ignore science at the price of irrelevance. Good religious thinking draws on all sources of truth, especially science, for if God did not "create" the world, God certainly operates in the world. (Personally, I think God creates the world every day.)

I would go further. The deeper our encounter with the world, scientific and not scientific, the better our religious thinking. It is no coincidence that Buber begins *I and Thou* by describing his encounter with a tree, or that Heschel develops the components of radical amazement—awe and wonder—to reinterpret and renew the Jewish relationship with God.

The spiritual action is right here.

RABBI PAUL KIPNES

1

God is not a being; God is a verb. Jewish tradition understands God's four-letter name as a meaningful combination of three verbs: *hei-vav-hei* (הוה), or *hoveh* (הֹוֶה), signifying the present tense and meaning "is"; *hei-yod-hei* (היה), or *hayah* (הָיָה), meaning "was"; and *yod-hei-yod-hei* (יהיה), or *yih'yeh* (יִהְיֶה), meaning "will be." God is that which was, is, and will be forevermore. As we sing in the prayer *Adon Olam*, God is the sum total of existence. The issue is not whether we believe in God. It does not matter. Because God just Is–Was–Will Be. The question, instead, should be whether we are willing to open our eyes, our minds, and our hearts to the continuously sacred flow of Existence.

God is found everywhere in every moment. That's why the ancient Rabbis knew God as *HaMakom* (הַמָּקוֹם), "The Place," meaning God is in every place, everywhere. God is here, over there, up there (pointing skyward), down there (pointing earthward), in there (pointing inside you and me). Wherever we can stop focusing on ourselves and our own material needs and open our eyes to the reality and beauty surrounding us, we might find God. The kabbalists knew God as *Ein Sof* (אֵין סוֹף), "No End," because God is everywhere, the Essence that is without end. Moses found God on a mountaintop, and so can we. Miriam encountered God at the shores of the sea, and so can we. The

Levites—originally ritual singer/musicians—heard God in the sweet multi-instrument musicals they played and sang, and so can we. And the prophet Elijah experienced God in the still small voice within that spoke to him, and so can we.

My relationship with God is always in flux. Sometimes I feel closer to the Holy One; sometimes farther away. There have been times when I have felt estranged from God. During my "rationalist" phase, God was an idea, an ideal. During my "non-rationalist" period, the Source of Life was in each relationship, à la philosopher Martin Buber's "I-Thou." Sometimes the Maker of Peace is in my meditative breath. Other times the Almighty is the recipient of my anger. Yes, I have yelled at God, but that's okay; God can take it. How I view God changes year by year, and sometimes day by day. Nonetheless, God's reality has been and remains a constant in my life.

2

I imagine a conversation between Man and God.

Man: God, You created everything?

God: Yes, each creation has its own purpose. Some of it blessedly benevolent; some of it potentially dangerous. Think about lions. Leave them alone and they are just gorgeous creatures. Bother them, and look out!

Man: What about earthquakes, tornados, and other natural disasters? Why did You create those?

God: Call these the dreadful consequence of an imperfect Creation. Call it collateral damage of My desire to create humanity. Natural disasters and unnatural disease were unintended; they weren't in any plan. Setting out to create, I began with exactness and perfection. But when I began creating the universe, I failed to realize that I was creating something that was other-than-Me. And because it was other-than-Me, it was imperfect. All approximations are intrinsically imperfect.

Man: So You created all those diseases—Alzheimer's, AIDS, and cancerous tumors that ravage our bodies and that cause children to die young and others to suffer so intensely?

God: Unintended for sure, but eminently treatable. I give you humans big brains and teach you to understand science and medicine. Then you must decide whether to focus your time and research dollars on curing diseases like cancer or Alzheimer's or if to use your God-given resources instead to build sophisticated smart bombs and laser-guided missiles.

Man: So You admit responsibility for evil and suffering?

God: I prefer to focus on My efforts to provide humanity with the ability to lessen suffering. Since earthquakes are unintended but inevitable, you humans have knowledge of them. In fact, all new homeowners in California sign a form acknowledging that they will be living near an earthquake fault and that they understand the danger.

Still, given the whole "free choice" component built into Creation, everyone (in theory) gets to decide how to live and where to live. With free choice, you humans have the freedom to make your own decisions—even dangerous and foolish ones. Imperfection allows humans to be greedy, to be cruel, or to ignore the responsibility to help and heal each other. Collectively, you humans have the ability to cure all these diseases and curb all evil. Do you also have the inclination to make it the priority?

3

God *is* the Eternal yardstick against which we measure ourselves. Torah—both the written scroll and the literature that grows out of it—serves as the wellspring from which our ethical values flow. When we study Torah, and the commentators, and the writings of teachers of each generation, we begin to understand the ethical imperatives of life. Our role in life—as Jews who struggle with God—is to determine what *imitatio Dei* (imitation of God) means.

God wanted to give us life. Like a parent, God brought us into this world so we could love and dream and bring joy to each other and to God. And God gave us minds to think and hands to work and hearts to lead with compassion. Some of us forget and think we are invincible. Or think it's only about us. And so we end up hurting ourselves and often hurting others in the process.

God wants us to learn from each loss. Learn to buckle up, to visit the doctor more often, to play safely. Stop sweating the small stuff, and fighting and kvetching. God, the Source of All Goodness, invites us to count our blessings more regularly. And to get good grades and do good work, so we can use our amazing minds to repair our world, to create great manifestations of our shared compassion and justice. God want us to speak truth to power, to speak love to pain, to make sure everyone can be healthy. We should give *tzedakah*, and repair our broken relationships before it is too late. You can invite God into your life by acting humbly, and living ethically, and caring for everyone, whether you know them or not.

We must live up to the best that we can be. And spend time with the ill ones, bringing them comfort amid their suffering. And never forget that the Eternal your God is always here: caring, loving, listening, holding us, and helping us through.

4

Of the seventy names for God referred to in Torah, *HaMakom*, meaning "The Place," speaks mostly loudly to me. Why do we call God "The Place," *HaMakom*? It's a metaphor. As physical beings, we sometimes best understand difficult concepts from a physical frame of reference. If we think about the meaning of a "place," we may agree that it is more than just a geographical location. A place is a space that is capable of containing something else. When we call God *HaMakom*, we mean that everything is contained within God, while God is not contained in anything. As our Sages say, "God does not have a place, rather God is The Place . . . of the Universe" (*B'reishit Rabbah* 68:9).

Have you ever been so overwhelmed by the beauty of nature surrounding you that you lost track of time, of priorities, of yourself? That is God. *HaMakom*.

In that first week following his creation, after the work of naming the animals, what did Adam do? *Midrash Tanchuma* tells us that Adam spent his free time admiring the glory of Creation. Overwhelmed to his very core, Adam stood silent on the shores of the sea, contemplating the majesty around him. Then he lifted up his voice to extol God, saying, מַה־רַבּוּ מַעֲשֶׂיךָ יְיָ (*Mah rabu maasecha Adonai*), "How great are Your works, O Eternal Creator!" (*Tanchuma*, *P'kudei* 3 to Psalm 104:24).

Adam responded with astonishment, and with deep appreciation. Then he became philosophical. In both the simple beauty of the ocean and in the world's complexity, Adam saw evidence of the Holy One. Philosophers call this panentheism, with the world being in God and God being in the world. The kabbalists, Jewish mystics, call this *Ein Sof*, that there is no end to the Holy One. God is everywhere. I just call it *HaMakom*.

Every inch of our world is flowing with its own flavors of milk and honey. Some of us see it. Many of us miss it. The prophet Isaiah said it best: *M'lo kol haaretz kvodo* (מְלֹא כָל הָאָרֶץ כְּבוֹדוֹ), "The whole world is filled with the Creator's magnificence" (Isaiah 6:3). God created. God sustains. God is. Here. In this place. The Place. *HaMakom*. This is God.

RABBI ZOE KLEIN

1

God as Creator, Parent, Shepherd, Judge, Love. We all have metaphors that speak to us. Metaphor is very personal, and potentially redemptive. As I've grown, my concept of God as "Author of All Metaphor" has deepened. I now believe that God is a Fiction Writer.

Some theologians assert that God is truth and everything else is falsehood. I disagree. I believe God is truth and everything else is fiction. Fiction differs greatly from falsehood. The world is a story spoken into being by, about, and for God. At the center of this exquisite poetic and tragic adventure is covenant.

Fiction is a key that opens the locked chambers of the heart. Linguistic purists claim that metaphor is a parasite, that what "my love is a red, red rose" really says is there are no words to express what I mean, so I will take words out of context and abuse them to express myself.

What they call untrue, I call revelation. Metaphor says, "I have no other means of language to express my feelings and fears, my creativity and my intellect, my sense of spiritual connectedness . . . I have a million thoughts and ideas and questions that I could unload over hours and hours, or I can simply admit the shortcomings of language and in my *desperation* to communicate, simply say everything in one easy breath: 'Man is a passing breeze.'"

In nonfiction, there is little need for relationship; but with metaphor, we must assume an intricate understanding based on trust. Metaphor relies on the ability for any two people to immediately begin a relationship.

The definition of metaphor is the conditional relationship of two concepts, a relationship between two nouns that is reciprocal. Both influence and redefine each other. Covenant is also a conditional, reciprocal relationship between two parties.

Stories reach deeply into hearts and minds because unlike nonfiction, demanding fractional attention, fiction invites our presence wholly: mind, body, spirit. It sweeps us away and returns us renewed with keener vision. We do not live objectively. We live in metaphor. Poetry does not just "make pretty." It reveals and it redeems. God is the Author of All Metaphor.

Before the universe came into being, God had no means to know that God existed. There was nothing against which to compare Godself. No mirror, just blank infinity. Then came the brilliant moment God realized "I am." Creation exploded into being with God's next thought. "I am what?" The Hebrew word for "what" and "matter" is the same: *mah* (מָה). We matter. We are God's story, the reflection through which God understands Godself.

God is a Fiction Writer, and fiction, ironically, is Ultimate Truth's master key.

2

I imagine that God weeps at the sufferings of the whole disharmonious natural world. If God does weep with us, it is with a heart that we wrote into the story. We invented God's heart, our greatest contribution to God's tale.

I cannot know why suffering and evil exist. No work of fiction is free of it. It is the stuff of timeless story. However, our greatest spiritual resistance to suffering is metaphor and interpretation. To interpret is divine. God breathed that ability into us.

A traditional Jewish ritual response to nightmares is called "the Amelioration of a Dream" (Babylonian Talmud, *B'rachot* 55b). The ritual requires three friends to declare that the dream be interpreted for good. The text explains that all dreams have a hint of prophecy; however, all dreams can be interpreted positively. In fact, the prophecy of the dream lies partially in its interpretation. The dreamer says three times, "אֲדֹנָי שָׁמַעְתִּי וְיָרֵאתִי," *Adonai shamati v'yareiti*—God, I heard what You made me hear and I was frightened. Three friends respond with the prescribed words, "Choose life, for God has already approved your deeds. Repentance, prayer, and charity remove the evil of the decree."

We dream, but we are also dreamt. We are written, and within that story, we write. It is said in Torah and our liturgy: "וּבַיּוֹם הַשְּׁבִיעִי שָׁבַת וַיִּנָּפַשׁ," *U'vayom hash'vi-i shavat vayinafash*, "On the seventh day God 'rested.'" Translators struggle in translating *vayinafash*, suggesting, "On the seventh day God rested and was refreshed." *Vayinafash*, however, literally means God "ensouled." On the seventh day God rested and created spirits. Out of God's dark, void chamber before Creation, God suddenly dreamed a dream/nightmare and based on that dream/nightmare, the world was sketched and animated in full color. We are the dream/nightmare. We have little control over the outcome except to interpret it for the good.

A congregant had a double mastectomy and did not know how to love herself afterwards. She would stand before a mirror naked, seeing herself as grotesque. We sought a metaphor that would help her to see herself in a new light. We imagined her body as a sacred altar and that her breasts were the sacrifices that redeemed her life. Years later she told me that now when she stands before the mirror, she thinks "sacred altar" and has found a love for herself inside that she thought had disappeared. She reinterpreted her nightmare through metaphor.

3

I believe in God as Author of All Life, yet I live as if God is *Reader* of All Life. The difference is profound. We wake each morning to a pristine day, an open page, and our actions are stylus and papyrus.

Every day, our response to God's story is inked in heartbeats, lettered in breath, rolled into a perfumed scroll, and tucked into the crook of an ancient oak tree. The way I live my life is my narrative and commentary, tossed up into the vast, churning literature of conch shells and migrating birds and spiraling galaxies.

Many others believe that God is the Source of Ethical Values, the Moral Compass. I do not sense that our ethics come from some Outside Other. I think God is the Writer of this strange fiction in which we are the characters playing out our moral dramas. It is not that I think God doesn't *care*, although I hesitate to assign human emotions to that which I cannot comprehend. The most I can say is that the story God has written is of great interest to God. God studies the world, gazes upon God's reflection in it. Just as we try to emulate what we imagine is God's will (essentially our own fiction writing), God also tries to emulate us. In other words, our morality comes from inside of us. It is not God's rule; it is our gift to God. It is our rebellion against the cruelty of coldness of the violent, ever-bleeding natural world—that despite the constancy of death, despite the sword that hangs over my head, I will interpret this for good, and I will live my life as a love letter to God. I perform mitzvot, and they are a serenade to the Author. My religion is not to be believed; it is to be danced. Every life is a once-told tale. Your story is a scripture, and God is the Reader; therefore, we are swept up in a cosmic love affair, whether God cares or not. Despite the nightmare, I will interpret for good and seal this Book of Life with a kiss.

O Reader of All Life, wait for me while I am away in battle on earth. I will write every day, and when I return I shan't leave You again. My actions are a love letter to You.

Read it, and weep.

4

The very first verse of Torah is grammatically problematic. The first word, *b'reishit* (בְּרֵאשִׁית), literally means "In the beginning of." The "of" presents a problem because it is not followed by a noun. Some translations leave a blank, an ellipses: "in the beginning of . . . God created heaven and earth." I love the blank. In the beginning of *what*? What is this, who are we, where are we going? I would prefer to keep the mystery than to massage the text, forcing it to click.

There is something more remarkable about the word *b'reishit* than its mysterious grammar. The question of whether the universe had a beginning in time has been debated for centuries. Aristotle believed that the world existed forever. Immanuel Kant believed time continued backward forever. For over four thousand years, Torah has opened with the radical word *b'reishit*, "In the beginning of."

In 1929, Edwin Hubble discovered that galaxies are moving away from us, that the universe is expanding. This meant that at some earlier time everything was closer together, and ten or twenty thousand million years ago, everything was in exactly the same place. Everything was one, infinitesimally small, and infinitely dense. Hubble replaced the stable state theory, which said that the universe was infinite, with the big bang theory, where time and space have a beginning.

What was before the beginning? "Rabbi Yonah said in Rabbi Levi's name: Why was the world created with the letter *bet* (ב)? The *bet* is closed at the sides but open in the front, preventing you from investigating what is above and below, what is before and behind" (*B'reishit Rabbah* 1:10).

Examining only the very first word of Torah, we might begin to answer this question by saying: yes, God has a role in nature and in history. There is a beginning, which implies a journey. Where we are going and God's role in nature and history are mysteries. The Torah begins with the second letter of the alphabet, the first is the silent *alef* (א), indicating that anything before the beginning is eternally mysterious to us. The world stands on mystery.

Perhaps God is not just a Fiction Writer but a Writer of Mystery and Suspense. History is a Choose Your Own Adventure novel. Only the Author knows where each plotline will lead, how it all ends, and the motives, ultimately, of whoever dunnit.

RABBI JASON ROSENBERG

1

What is the relationship between you and the cells of your body?

From one perspective, you are made up entirely of your cells. You are nothing except for a conglomeration of these microscopic building blocks. That's fairly obvious when we think about our physical selves, but even our minds—our thoughts and feelings—exist in our brains, which are made up of cells. If you take away all of my cells, you have taken away all of me—there would be nothing left.

Of course, it is obvious that I am also more than my cells. The human being that exists is more complicated, more interesting, and more important than any number of these individual cells. When people meet me, they don't think about my cells. They think about *me*. They think about the gestalt—the larger entity that grows out of those cells. I am the larger reality that is made of, but transcends, the individual cells that make up my body.

It's exactly the same as the relationship between individual bytes of data on a CD and music. From one, narrow perspective, there is nothing except for the data on a CD. But, when brought together, a larger, transcendent reality emerges—the data comes together and becomes music.

The relationship between my cells and my self is the relationship between the data and the music.

And, it's the same as the relationship between everything and God.

God is not some being, some entity who is "out there" somewhere. God is not some Other for whom I can look and, if I'm lucky enough, with whom I can have a relationship. God is the larger, transcendent reality that grows out of the entirety of creation. Everything is God. God is everything, and more.

When I was younger, I had a more conventional theology, but it couldn't hold up to scrutiny. As a devout rationalist, there are, quite frankly, too many problems, too many flaws in that kind of theology. And, I'm dedicated to a religious life that requires no abdication of the mind. My God has to be one in whom I can believe with my head, as well as my heart. As my rabbi, Jerome Malino (*z"l*) used to say, believing in something that you know to not be true isn't faith; it's blind faith, and it's nothing of which to be proud.

This is a God who doesn't try to exist despite the facts before us. This is a God who grows out of them and transcends them. Everything is God.

2

What is God's relationship to suffering and evil?

There isn't one.

When most people talk about God's relationship to suffering and evil, they're talking about causation—why would a God who is all-good and all-powerful allow terrible things to happen? And, for those who hold a more traditional, dualist theology (that is, those who believe that God is some Other), it's a serious, troubling question. Why would a God such as that choose not to help those in need? It might be understandable when it comes to human acts of evil—if free will is given, it must be given fully, or it's not given at all. But, when it comes to "natural" suffering, it's harder to understand. Why wouldn't an all-powerful God cure, for example, childhood cancer? And, more troubling to me, why would anybody worship a God who could, but refuses to do so?

Of course, to the non-dualist, to someone who believes that God is not "out there," but rather that we are all part of a larger, transcendent God, there is no question at all. God does not "do" anything. God cannot act in the world in the way that we can. So, asking why God allows these things is a non sequitur. Analogies here are so limited, but it's a little bit like asking why music doesn't stop bad songs from happening. The question doesn't even make sense.

Of course, in different ways, God still has a relationship with suffering and evil. After all, God has a relationship with everything, by definition. It starts to make sense when we remember that God is not made up of each and every individual thing, independently. God is made up of—God grows out of, really—the interconnectedness of all things. God is the larger pattern that emerges from it all. And so, where there is a lack of connection, where there is a brokenness, there is (if we can even say such a thing) a lack of God.

When something terrible happens, when someone acts evilly toward another, or when someone is suffering, there is less connectedness. And, in those times and places, God is less manifest in the world. The more we can reconnect, the more we can fix what is broken, the more we make God real again.

Where there is suffering and evil, God isn't.

3

Once again, it's clear that to a non-dualist, there isn't a simple, direct connection between God and ethical values. God did not "command" certain ethical behaviors of us, in the way in which most people would understand "command." But, there is clearly a connection between God and ethical values.

Much like the question of suffering and evil, God's relationship to ethics comes down to interconnectedness. God is found, God is manifest, in the interconnectedness of all things in our world. The more connection, the more God. When we act in ethical ways, we are strengthening the bonds between and among us. Every kind act I do for someone makes me feel more connected to them. It makes me realize that I am responsible for them. And, every time someone does something for me, I can experience that as a manifestation of their own sense of responsibility and connectedness. Ethical behavior is, in essence, "applied connectedness." It is connectedness, played out in the real world. And so, by revealing and strengthening our connections, ethical behavior reveals and strengthens our awareness of God. It might, if we dare say such a thing, make God more real in the world.

What's fascinating to me is that this relationship works in reverse, as well. Not only does ethical behavior make us more aware of God, but awareness of God makes us more ethical. When I seek God, I do so by seeking out connection. And so, it's almost inevitable that that seeking will result in my feeling more connected to other people, as well. In that sense, connection will, of course, lead to more ethical behavior.

Author Jay Michaelson, in writing about the reliability of mystical experiences, teaches that every great mystical tradition in world history has used "kindness toward others" as one of the, if not the, major criteria for evaluating our religious experiences (Michaelson, "Does Mysticism Prove the Existence of God?"). If you come out of a religious experience *not* feeling kinder and more obligated to your fellow humans, then by definition it wasn't a true religious experience. True religious experiences *always* lead to stronger ethical impulses. True religion and moral, ethical behavior are so intertwined as to be inseparable.

Ethical behavior leads to an awareness of God. An awareness of God leads to ethical behavior.

I don't think that's an accident.

4

In a non-dualist system, God cannot have any active role in the natural world or in human history. God did not "create" the world in the way that I might create a sculpture. God does not influence history in the way that a powerful person can.

But, history and nature can reveal God.

The complexity of our world, on every level from subatomic through geopolitical, is breathtaking. It is, in the original, religious sense, Awesome. Awe-inspiring. And, one of the primary goals of religion is to draw our intention to that Awesome interconnectedness.

Take, for example, the seemingly simple act of eating a piece of bread. Normally, we don't think much about it; it's just bread. But, that bread has within it hints of an infinitely complex world. The bread comes from grain, which is a plant, which grows through the process of photosynthesis. Of course, photosynthesis only happens because of sunlight, which only happens because of nuclear fusion in the sun. The plant also needs soil to grow, which brings in a whole other complex network of science. And, of course, the bread got to the supermarket on a truck, which was powered by gasoline, which comes from oil, which comes from dead dinosaurs. So, eating a piece of bread is, with the proper *kavanah* (כַּוָּנָה), "intention," a reference to molecular biology, fusion, geology, paleontology, and more. Arguably, the entirety of science is contained within a single piece of bread.

At its best, a simple prayer like *HaMotzi* is meant to draw our attention to that larger, sublime reality. God did not create that piece of bread, in the simple sense of that statement. But all of God's glorious interconnectedness was necessary for the bread to exist. And so, properly contemplated, a simple piece of bread can reveal God.

Human history is no less complex. The smallest act can have outsized and unknowable consequences, even at a great distance away and much later in time. I cannot tell you precisely how, but I know that our entire world is, on every level, interconnected in an infinitely complex way. When I contemplate that, it leaves me feeling ever so slightly shaken. Awestruck.

Like I'm in the presence of some One greater than myself.

RABBI ARIANA SILVERMAN

1

It is incredible that a connection to God permeates every moment of my life—from cries of despair to shouts of ecstasy—and yet this intimate, ever-present experience is impossible to describe. We, as human beings, are limited by our language and symbols and frameworks, and we are limited by the particular cultural and historical context in which we live. We must use limited tools to describe the limitless.

And yet I am compelled to write about God because I worry that fear of talking about God prevents Jews from realizing the diversity of thought about God that is authentically Jewish. I am disheartened by how many Jews think that the only legitimate understanding of God is the man-on-a-throne image presented in the Bible and, to some extent, in Rabbinic literature. That is the understanding of God with which I grew up, and only as an adult have I come to realize that view is only one perspective.

It should come as no surprise that my understanding of God has evolved, because if I still believed what I did as a child, that would be a disservice to God. Everything else in my life has evolved—what I eat, where I live, what I know, who is in my family and my most intimate circle of friends.

But the anthropomorphic understanding of a male God has perhaps been the hardest thing to let go. And so when I am confronted with the biblical or liturgical texts that present such a view of God, there is a guilt that emerges—how do I know that my understanding of God has evolved in the right way? Am I smart enough, sensitive enough—Jewish enough—to have an authentic experience?

Perhaps the best I can do is to give examples of where and when I experience the Divine. God inspires my pursuit of social justice. God is the power that makes me, in the words of one of my teachers, tremble with prophetic rage.

I perceive God when I am confronted with the awesome beauty and complexity of the natural world. And it is that beauty that helps me to experience God in amazement and gratitude.

I experience God in Jewish study and stories. The process of engaging with that wisdom is a form of sacred relationship with God. I believe the Torah teaches us truths about the world in which we live. And so do our teachers—from the Rabbis of the Talmud to twentieth-century theologians to the scholars of our time.

And I feel God's presence in human relationships. Recognizing the sacred in one another. The love and laughter that bring joy to our lives.

2

Suffering and evil clearly exist in the world. Our challenge as Jews is to determine how to respond. We may never know *why* suffering occurs, but we must ask what we do when suffering occurs and how what we do reflects who we are.

And God is deeply involved in that process. In the vein of predicate theology, regardless of whether an interventionist God heals the sick, healing the sick is godly. We elevate the sacred when we work toward *shalom*, toward wholeness.

And when we are in pain, God is with us, whether we know it or not. During one of the darkest times in my life, even though I did not necessarily believe that God had caused my pain, I was angry and feared that anger would destroy my relationship with God. At the time, God and I were barely on speaking terms. I could not pray. I had no interest in study. I questioned why I had devoted my life to a sacred but painful calling. But I realized that even in those moments of deep suffering, my relationship with God did not disappear. And no matter how sad or angry I became, a consciousness of God remained. I made a discovery that saved my faith. I realized it is perfectly okay to be angry with God.

And after the cycles of screaming and silence, when I wanted to start speaking again, I was paralyzed by an inability to pray. So I sought the teaching of my Hebrew Union College–Jewish Institute of Religion liturgy professor Lawrence Hoffman. Following his advice, I started by picking one prayer/blessing to say. Just one. And I stuck with it for a while, until I could say two. And as I pieced together the diversity of words we use to engage with God, I learned that God is more complex and more whole than I ever knew. And, perhaps, God is the power that compels us to choose life.

My gratitude returned with the crocuses. After that painful winter, I was startled one day to discover shoots of green and purple emerging from the frozen ground. And I learned what it really means to pray the words of *Modah Ani.* I felt my soul had been restored, and I was grateful. There was nothing more beautiful and breathtaking than the discovery of bursts of color and life emerging from the earth and in me.

3

Living in relationship with God helps me in my striving to become the person I want to be. When I am cognizant of the inherent interconnectedness and oneness of life, when I see the divine in the other, I am dissuaded from acting in a way that ignores that oneness. I recognize that my life is not whole when another person's is broken. And I am motivated not by some future reward, but by a desire to do what is right for its own sake.

And as I have immersed myself more deeply in Jewish learning and living, I have become more passionate about justice and more compassionate in my relationships. However, I do not believe the mitzvot and halachah are intended solely to make you a better person. Some are ethical imperatives, but many are ritual or theological. Judaism is about more than ethics. It is a framework for sacred living. But intentional engagement with our tradition can deepen our understanding of our obligation to pursue justice.

When Hillel stated that what is hateful to you, do not do to another person, he concluded by stating, "Now go and study." It is this latter part that is often forgotten when the story is cited, but it is critical. Part of living an ethical life is recognizing the importance of striving to learn from our texts and our teachers.

Before I went to work for the Religious Action Center of Reform Judaism (RAC) as an environmental advocate, I was already passionate about environmental protection and human rights. But when I began wrestling more deeply with God and with Jewish texts and teachers, I developed a language and foundation that transformed my ability and commitment to be a steward of the sacredness of life and a prophetic voice in partnership with those fighting for environmental justice.

Does a relationship with God and immersion in Jewish teaching always make you a better person? Not always. But reverence for that which is eternal and life-affirming, coupled with active analytical engagement with evolving Jewish wisdom, can guide and strengthen us. If God is the interconnectedness of all things, we affirm life through ethical living.

4

Stories are vital to our understanding of the world. The stories we tell, and the way we tell them, help us to learn who we are. When I look at the story of Creation, for example, it is less important to me whether history unfolded exactly as described. Instead, I am fascinated by what we mean when we use this story to think about the basis for and wonder of life. Even if we do not believe that an interventionist God created the world in six days and rested on the seventh or parted the sea so that we could walk to freedom, there is a "truth" in our stories.

A Jicarilla Apache creation narrative begins, "In the beginning nothing was here where the world now stands; there was no ground, no earth—nothing but Darkness, Water, and Cyclone" (Opler, *Myths and Tales of the Jicarilla Apache Indians*, 1). Genesis begins, "When God began to create heaven and earth—the earth being unformed and void, with darkness over the surface of the deep and a wind from God sweeping over the water." Even if the similarities in these stories from peoples thousands of miles apart do not reflect a historical or scientific truth about creation, what they tell us about our connection as human beings to each other and to the planet on which we live remains deeply, even scientifically, true.

I believe we can see and experience God's presence in the natural world. When I was sixteen, I participated in OSRUI's (Olin Sang Ruby Union Institute) four-week backpacking trip in Colorado and Utah. We took turns carrying a small Torah scroll in a waterproof bag as we climbed, hiked, and canoed. One Shabbat morning, we held our worship service on top of a mountain. As the rabbi lifted the scroll for *hagbah*, the sun shone through the parchment and the letters seemed to catch fire. And as I looked at this scroll and saw the rolling green peaks behind it, alive with endless brightly colored wildflowers and illuminated by that same light, I realized that it all was One. We are all part of a greater whole, an interconnected web of existence, and that interconnectedness is sacred. When I look at the world, I see the sacred in both the big and small—the grandeur of nature and the joy and love in human relationships. And as I have grown to recognize these experiences as experiences of the Divine and read the works of generations of scholars, I have realized that yes, my experience of God is authentic, and it is Jewish.

RABBI SUZANNE SINGER

1

My mother was a survivor of Auschwitz. This reality has been the major driving force in my life. Overriding all that I do, think, and feel has been my struggle with the question: "Why?" When I was younger, I was torn between two poles. Either I was very angry at God or I could not believe in God at all. If God intervened to free us from slavery in Egypt, why had not God intervened during the Holocaust? Either God did not care what happened to human beings or, at best, God was impotent or nonexistent. And if one chose to blame the Holocaust on people and free will, then how could God have created a world in which such evil is possible? God's inaction during the Holocaust brooked no excuses.

Emil Fackenheim offered as a 614th commandment that we are forbidden from giving Hitler a posthumous victory by abandoning Judaism. In theological terms, that meant I could not give up on God. In my struggle to come to terms with God, I studied many different theologies. I slowly came to understand that God was not necessarily the equivalent of the old man with a white beard, sitting on a celestial throne and running the world like a puppeteer. This freed me from my narrow conception of God and allowed me to embrace a new understanding of the Divine.

I resonated most with Mordecai Kaplan's belief that God is the "power that makes for salvation," the power that allows us to achieve our full potential as human beings and that drives us to bring justice and truth to the world (Kaplan, *The Radical American Judaism of Mordecai Kaplan*, 146). The God of the Bible is thus a metaphor. God is not a Being, but a Force; not a personal or providential God, but a Source from which to draw strength and inspiration. I realized that if I could open myself up to *this* God, I could become the person I was meant to be in the world. I no longer had to blame God for the Holocaust because that was no longer the kind of God I believed in or rejected. I understood that I was God's partner, co-responsible for perfecting the world.

Of course, there are still times that I revert to the notion of God as the old king in control, so I still get angry at Him on occasion. But who are we as Jews if not God-wrestlers, struggling to know and to respond to God, struggling to understand why we are here?

2

The suffering of so many innocent people in the world has troubled me my whole life, beginning with the experiences of my mother and her family, through the many holocausts that have continued to occur around the world, and the poverty and abuse to which so many are subjected. If God is the force for salvation, why are more people not saved? If God is only associated with the good, does that not let God off the hook? One of my greatest challenges has been to satisfactorily resolve the problem of theodicy—reconciling an all-good and all-powerful God with the existence of evil.

Eugene Borowitz and Harold Kushner have both suggested that God's power is limited, and it seems to me that this is the only possible resolution of this dilemma. The speeches from the whirlwind in the Book of Job illustrate this beautifully. In them, God gives Job a sweeping view of the universe's magnificence, making it clear that at best, God keeps the forces of evil—symbolized by Behemoth, the land monster, and Leviathan, the sea monster—at bay.

As intellectually satisfying as this solution has been to me, however, there are still times when my doubts take hold. Irving "Yitz" Greenberg has suggested that after Auschwitz, we must be able to defend our theology "in the presence of the burning children" (Greenberg, "Cloud of Smoke, Pillar of Fire," 23). I subscribe to Greenberg's understanding of "moment faiths"—times when we can believe in God's redeeming power, and times when we simply cannot. If there are no atheists in foxholes, there are atheists when confronted with the reality of devastated lives.

It is comforting to some to believe that God rewards us for our good deeds and punishes us for our transgressions. It gives people a sense of control over their lives. In my view, God does neither. We suffer either because of the consequences of our own actions or because God's redeeming power has not yet overcome the force of chaos. Several instances in our tradition feature God crying over the fate of God's people. The prophet Jeremiah quotes, "If you do not heed me, I will hide and I will weep because of your arrogance. I will cry and cry, My eyes will flow with tears because My flock has been taken into captivity" (Jeremiah 13:17). In a midrash on Lamentations, God cries twice over the destruction of the Jerusalem Temple (*Eichah Rabbah*, proem/*p'tichta* 24). When we suffer, I like to think that God is crying along with us.

3

I do not believe in a personal God, but I feel commanded by God where ethics are concerned. I believe that God demands I engage in the repair of the world. A midrash illustrates my point. The Israelites are about to receive the Ten Commandments at Sinai. The Hebrew text literally reads that they are standing "under" the mountain (*b'tachtit*, בְּתַחְתִּית Exodus 19:17). The Talmud surmises, "This teaches us that the Holy One inclined the mountain over them like a tilted barrel and that God said, 'If you accept the Torah, all is well; if not, here will be your grave'" (Babylonian Talmud, *Shabbat* 88a)—in other words, God will drop the mountain on your heads. When I first heard this interpretation, I was incensed. God imposes the Torah on the Jewish people under penalty of death? I thought we were given free will.

Emmanuel Levinas helped me to understand this interpretation as conveying the true meaning of being in covenant with God. For Levinas, Torah equals ethics. He believes that the Torah's fundamental teaching is that we are infinitely responsible for other people. This is why the Torah constantly mandates that we love our neighbor and even the stranger, that we feed the hungry and clothe the naked. In the realm of ethics, Levinas's God offers us absolutely no choice. In fact, Levinas says, we do not choose the Torah; rather, it is the Torah that chooses us.

Levinas thus explains the midrash on the mountain as follows (Levinas, *Nine Talmudic Readings*, 41): The Rabbis believe that God created this world so that the ethical order could be fulfilled. The Torah is our blueprint for accomplishing this mission. If we reject the Torah, the world loses its meaning and reverts to chaos. Creation is annihilated. We must accept our election to lead lives of Torah or witness the destruction of the world. Furthermore, Levinas believes that the Torah's ethics are not simply obligations but are essential to who we are as human beings. It is only by adhering to the Torah's ethics that we can reach our full God-given potential. We ignore the Torah's precepts at the risk of losing our humanity.

To be a Jew is to have stood at Sinai, personally receiving and accepting the Torah. As Jews, we begin our journey in a covenantal relationship with God. Our commitment to Torah is a kind of preexisting condition, one that limits our choices and our freedom. We must take responsibility for one another, or the tilted barrel of egotism and callousness will drop on our heads.

4

Belief in God does not contradict science because science and theology are responding to very different concerns. Science explains how and why things work as they do. Theology and religion give meaning to our lives. God is not a supernatural Being who performs miracles that upend the laws of physics. Miracles are about our paying attention to what occurs in nature and uncovering the potential beneath the surface. Being mindful about our surroundings, we can connect with the Power, or the Ground of Being, that is, God, and discern the path that will prove to be redemptive.

For example, I do not believe that God literally split the Sea of Reeds (Exodus 14:21). Rather, it is possible that when the Israelites prepared to cross the Sea of Reeds, the sea was at low tide, exposing an elevated stretch of sand that had been submerged in water. Low tide occurred every day, of course, but it was not until Moses noticed this phenomenon that he found an escape route from Egypt. Moses's faith in God as Redeemer allowed him to preserve the hope that a way out could be found.

In the same vein, I do not believe that God literally intervenes in history to change its course. Rather, people must come to the point where they believe that redemption is possible. An alcoholic does not commit to recovery until he or she is ready to accept help. Before that, he or she is in denial and will not engage in *t'shuvah* (תְּשׁוּבָה), "repentance." This is how I understand the verse in Exodus telling us that "God heard their [the Israelites'] moaning, and God remembered the covenant with Abraham and Isaac and Jacob" (Exodus 2:24). This verse is disturbing if we believe in a God who intervenes in history, because we must ask: Why didn't God respond sooner? Why did God wait four hundred years to remember this covenant? But if God is the Power of Salvation, then you can understand this verse as indicating that the people finally realized they were oppressed and were ready to be free. You might say they experienced a revolutionary wake-up call. Only then could they believe in the possibility of a different life, only then could they discover the hidden blessings in their surroundings (e.g., the meteorological and environmental changes that caused the Nile to turn red, the frogs to leap out of the river, and so on, causing fear in Pharaoh and the Egyptians), and only then could they take the necessary steps to embark on their journey to freedom.

RABBI LANCE SUSSMAN

1

"I believe in God" are not words I could have easily uttered until rather recently in my life. As a teenager and then as a college student, I regularly wrestled with the concept of God with little success. Struggling with the idea of God was my main religious activity for many years. By contrast, my desire to learn Hebrew and learn to participate in traditional Jewish worship was more intellectual and ethnic. While those interests ebbed and flowed over time, coming up with a meaningful definition of God and embracing it was constant.

For many years I persuaded myself as a congregational rabbi who led services regularly to transcend questions of belief and to read with feeling, hoping that the principle of *naaseh v'nishma* (נַעֲשֶׂה וְנִשְׁמָע, doing leads to understanding) would result in a higher spiritual unity. My more theologically astute congregants were well aware of my dilemma, and as one older gentleman, a Polish Holocaust survivor who shared many of his own doubts, once said to me, "Rabbi, your problem is that you have the head of an atheist and the heart of a Chasid," and, he added, "and that's why we get along." Around the same time, I learned a saying attributed to various religious virtuosos: "Anyone can argue about God, but no one argues with kindness." For the time being, I was content with a predicate theology, the position that it is okay to be godly, with or without God.

The years passed. I gained life experience. I spent a great deal of time studying different concepts of God. Each added a refinement to my view of God, but none served as the final piece in my God puzzle.

The intellectual wall I built around God was finally breached unexpectedly while I was reading a book by Erich Fromm, who challenged and reassured me that at a certain point radical monotheism necessarily becomes a species of atheism. At one point, Y'hudah HaLevi's admonition that "we cannot know God because that would be an imperfection in God, but we can still know that there is a God" made sense to me. God now was at least an existential/realistic possibility for me.

What was missing in my religious equation was a God of the heart. That moment came for me in a hospital when one of our children was misdiagnosed with a terminal cancer. Upon hearing the news, I found myself leaning headfirst on a wall asking God to spare him and us from a death sentence that literally came out of nowhere. I immediately realized what happened (my dad, a World War II veteran, also maintained a lifelong trench theology) and allowed myself a bittersweet smile. I know many desperate prayers are not answered, but now I knew what it meant to cry out in pain to a cosmic court of appeal. Today, while I have a definition of God—namely, the transcendent Source of being, goodness, and hope—my theology would still not fill a thimble. For now, a little bit of faith in a listening God is good enough for me

2

Three years ago, I started teaching a course in Holocaust and art in my synagogue's Confirmation Academy. I begin with a discussion of "Art and Suffering." Because of Christianity, Western art has long featured suffering as redemptive, with images of a crucified Jesus and a grieving Mary as powerful representations of the power of grief and love, both human and divine. Eternal suffering, on the other hand, is viewed as just punishment for the damned. By contrast, biblical authors and

Rabbinic writers mostly understand the national suffering of the Jewish people, including the destruction of the Temple and enduring exile, as purposeful suffering, and individual damnation as eternal extinction but not suffering.

For modern Jews of all religious stripes, none of the classical explanations of suffering are even remotely valid. On the one hand, the idea of exile as a national punishment has largely been replaced with a view of Diaspora as nonpunitive and personal extinction as scientifically probable and definitely not a divine punishment. Moreover, attempts to find an alternative in the Book of Job to explain either suffering or evil come up short. In Job, suffering is allowed by God. Ultimately the message that I read in Job is for us simply "to deal with it."

The closest any current theological position comes to explaining suffering in a satisfactory fashion is expressed by Rabbi Harold Kushner in his popular book *When Bad Things Happen to Good People.* In the end, Kushner makes the case for a loving but less than omnipotent Deity who listens to our pleas but ultimately is unable to intervene in human affairs.

At the pastoral level, I try to refrain from any language involving God as a micromanager or any attempt to defend God as loving, good, and the ultimate guarantor of only good outcomes. Similarly, I cringe at the recent wave of hospital television advertisements that promise wonderful outcomes for all their cancer and cardiac patients. Instead, I am forced back onto a predicate theology and try to be a good listener and an empathetic presence. Often, that is enough.

3

While the "ethical monotheism" of former generations of Reform Jews has largely given way to various expressions of monotheistic ethnicity, many of the concerns of the Reform Movement remain essentially ethical. For example, the battles for gender equality and the normalization of multiple expressions of human sexuality have been anchored in religious discourse by the Reform rabbinate and have led to radical rereadings of our ancient texts. Moreover, so-called prophetic Judaism and its championing of the Civil Rights Movement has given way to an advocacy program for a wide spectrum of liberal causes and local charitable efforts, many of which now involve food insecurity.

An appetite for ethical discourse is still very much in evidence among Reform Jews today, with the concept of *tikkun olam* central to contemporary Reform Judaism. In a recent Torah study class, a group of my congregants grappled with the tension between the idea of an ethical core for all of humanity as expressed in the Noahide Laws (derived from Genesis 9:9) and the idea that Judaism has a unique ethic of its own. In the end, they were more comfortable with the idea of a national "social contract" than a God-sanctioned universal moral covenant and with the idea that Judaism is deeply ethical, but not necessarily unique, in its views.

What was missing from this conversation was any reference to Judaism's prophetic literature. This critical context for our ethical behavior is too often obscured from view by the religious narcissism of our age. Indeed, rational discourse on ethics combined with a close reading of Amos, Hosea, and other prophets is one of the foundational pieces of Reform Judaism historically, but is often missing today. The marginalization of the ethical is a disaster for Reform Judaism and perhaps all of humanity.

4

About twenty years ago I worked on a *d'var Torah* with a very bright bat mitzvah student who had been assigned *Parashat B'reishit*, the first reading in the Torah. We read Genesis 1 together, following which she told me that she did not believe one word of the Torah's account of Creation and that she was going to be a scientist. About ten years later, I bumped into the same student, who asked me to forgive her for what had transpired in my office. I assured her that was not necessary and that I was proud of her. "What are you doing now?" I asked her. "Studying for a PhD in astrophysics at Harvard," she replied, "the big bang and all that." I smiled.

Despite a few commercially successfully hard-core atheists like Richard Dawkins, I generally find that science and scientists have generally become softer on issues of human spirituality during the last two decades. Organized religion and God may still be the "bad guys" in some circles, but spirituality as a human characteristic seems to be more comprehensible and even slightly more acceptable. As human beings, the argument goes, we need to find meaning in life. Thus, dance, poetry, the visual arts, music, and more all have the capacity to express the human spirit and help us meet our need for transcendence and meaning.

In this scenario, there is little reason for modern religion to do battle with science. While a Reform luminary like Isaac Mayer Wise may have rejected evolution as unbiblical, contemporary Reform Judaism has no bone to pick with science. Science is about the physical universe and how we can understand it, harness it, and live in harmony with it. Science does not have the capacity to determine our ethics, our aesthetics, or our need to construct a cosmos of meaning for ourselves and humanity.

The relationship of science and religion has been re-traumatized in recent years. Today, as in the time of the Scopes Trial, Protestant fundamentalists are at war with science. In Judaism, the Orthodox have co-opted scientific method in their pursuit of perfect kashrut and have fought mightily to reconcile every word of Torah with science. To Reform Jews, both attempts seem oddly out of step with both science and religion.

For modern Jews, it is more than possible to read *B'reishit* and agree that the essential message is that life "is good," and there is order and majesty in the universe. That's the poetry of our faith soaring, not its science failing. Just ask my young astrophysicist.

RABBI ANDREW VOGEL

1

I was walking my dog on a pitch-black summer Cape Cod night a few years ago, unable to see a thing. Suddenly, my eyes adjusted, and I could see the whole array of stars lit up on the black dome of the sky, the Milky Way clear and visible to me, the blinking and twinkling of the stars glowing brightly like jewels in the sky. As my dog came and stood right next to me, there in the dark—whammo!—I had the sudden awareness: that the stars, emitting their light across tens of millions of light-years, traveling through time, past the evolution of humankind forty thousand years ago, past the rise and fall of the species, past the formation of the seas and the continents, the stars themselves just forming, just being born—all that energy and light had brought about the simple, quiet moment of my beloved dog and me, standing together, experiencing life together, having evolved from the same energy that created the stars billions of years ago. The whole universe—all time, all being, it seemed to me—*all* was breathing, shining, alive, one united whole.

At that moment, I petted my dog, and then I recited the *Sh'ma*. "Hear O Israel, the Eternal our God, the Eternal is One." The simple declaration that there is nothing but God: all Being is God, everything is One, everything is One, we are part of that Oneness, you and I—and my dog. This is the central theological teaching of our religion.

Once, I thought of God as *separate from*, or transcending, the world. The language of the Bible instilled in me the image of God as the Old Bearded Man in the Sky gruffly issuing commandments, angrily smiting people. As I grew older, I doubted that that God existed, because I had never experienced that God in my life. I questioned God's existence—but, truly, it was *that image* of God that I was rejecting. I still sensed a purpose to life, felt moral imperatives, and was amazed by the complexity of nature, of consciousness, of life and love and caring. Today, I see God as the process of the unfolding of evolution itself. God is immanent, within Creation, not apart from it—the becoming of Creation. Rabbi Arthur Green writes that it is that God who "dwells within (rather than who 'controls' or 'oversees') the evolutionary process is the One about which—or about Whom—we tell the great sacred tale, the story of existence" (Green, *Radical Judaism*, 17).

2

No one can wave away the problem of God's coexistence with the presence of evil and suffering in our world. Human suffering is too great, too vast, too universal, too painful; the evil that we humans have wreaked upon each other is overwhelming in its scope and destruction. Who can bear to accept God's toleration of the murder, torture, and destruction we have brought into our world?

But much depends on how we think of God. If I hope God will swoop down with a mighty arm and change everything, I will be disappointed in God. All life, all experience, is a manifestation of God. Suffering, much like love and caring, is part of life. Suffering is not a punishment. God is not distinct from all Being, so blaming God for the evil done to me gets me nowhere; it is like blaming the ocean for its rough waves on a stormy day.

Yet, the evolutionary process has implanted within the human spirit an urge to resist evil and the will for life and good to triumph. Healing, emerging from suffering, and the struggle against evil, I believe, are all terms that are synonymous with the word "God." We Jews refer to God as the *rofeih chol basar umafli laasot* (רוֹפֵא כָל בָּשָׂר וּמַפְלִיא לַעֲשׂוֹת)—roughly translated as "Healer of all creatures, who amazes us with unexpected deeds." If we are fortunate, surprising transformations can occur. Jewish tradition speaks of God as the possibility of healing and renewal, of hope: God is *mikveih Yisrael* (מִקְוֵה יִשְׂרָאֵל), the Hope of Israel (Jeremiah 14:8). The Passover Haggadah reminds us that it is not just a myth, but rather very possible, for us to move from "slavery to freedom, from despair to joy, from mourning to celebration, from darkness to light, from enslavement to redemption" (Rabinowicz, *Passover Haggadah: Feast of Freedom*, 69).

Not every story ends happily with healing and celebration, of course. Suffering is a very real part of life, it is beyond our control, and often there seems to be no reason for it. What we can control, however, is our own religious attitude in the world, our response to suffering and evil. "Behold, I set before you this day life and good, death and evil. . . . Choose life, that you might live" (Deuteronomy 30:15, 30:19). Our choices, like many paths at a crossroads, lie before us. Through choosing compassion, strength, memory, and perseverance, we affirm life and its mysterious holiness, in which God dwells.

3

People often cross ethical boundaries because they are wrapped up in their own egos, deluded into thinking that they are so important as to be the center of the universe, that they are the only beings that matter. All sorts of mischief usually ensues from this kind of thinking. Most often, when we become self-obsessed, we become selfish and lose our ability to be empathetic toward others.

When the infamous Nazi Eichmann said, "I was just following orders," he was denying an important truth about human responsibility. His statements repudiated the idea that no one is merely a "cog in the machine," that everyone is responsible for their acts, that human actions matter, that everything is connected. He denied the truth that All Being is One.

When we become aware of God as the totality of Being, we can see how connected all life is. In the 1980s, an international crew of astronauts was launched into space on the space shuttle *Discovery*, a crew that included Americans, French, and even Saudi astronauts. Reflecting on the unique perspective on human life that he gained from space, one of them said, "The first day or so [in space] we each pointed to our countries. The third or fourth day we were pointing to our continents. By the fifth day, we were aware of only one Earth" (Daley, "Earth to Mars: Choosing a Flag to Unite a Planet"). Awareness of the Oneness of all Being, of which we are a part, raises our compassion and our sense of ethical responsibility to all.

In his *Tikkun HaK'lali*, Rabbi Nachman of Bratzlav encouraged people struggling with their egos to recite certain chapters from the Psalms to help them reconnect with the greater Whole of life, namely, God. One of those chapters, Psalm 90, reminds us that our lives are short, compared to the time and space that God has created: "A thousand years in Your sight are like yesterday when they are past, or as a watch in the night" (Psalm 90:4). There's a correction for your ego: your entire lifespan is as short as a blink of God's eye! Realizing that we are nearly insignificant compared to God and the vastness of Creation isn't meant to squash us and our ego and leave us wallowing in nihilism; the psalm goes on to offer this prayer:, "Teach us to number our days, that we may achieve a heart of wisdom" (Psalm 90:12). We become wise realizing our human limitations, opening our hearts compassionately, and accepting our responsibilities to others.

4

Years ago, in my first months as the rabbi at my congregation in Boston, surrounded by universities, hospitals, law schools, and scientific research facilities, a peculiar conversation kept repeating itself. A parade of longtime synagogue members came to speak with me as we began to form our relationships together. Many of the conversations began in exactly the same way: "Rabbi, so nice to meet you, but I just want to tell you one thing before we get started: I don't believe in God." I appreciated their candor, but as the discussion continued I realized that the God they were rejecting was the same as the God that I, too, had rejected. They were stuck on the idea of God as a supernatural being, separate from the universe, a character with a personality (and a very unlikable personality, at that!).

Shifting the paradigm about how we understand God helps with a more meaningful conversation. God is, as the Jewish mystics taught, the totality of Being, unimaginable in its scope and depth. One of Judaism's names for God is spelled *Yod-Hei-Vav-Hei* (יהוה), an impossible combination of the past, present, and future tenses of the verb "to be" in Hebrew. A best approximation is to translate this as "is-was-will-be-ness." Although its meaning is close to the word "Being," it is more of an active word than a cold philosophical term like "Being"—better would be "Being-in-Becoming" (see Green, *Radical Judaism*).

The thirteenth-century kabbalist Rabbi Moshe de Leon understood God in a way that especially resonates with a scientist's description of the big bang: "The beginning of existence is the secret concealed point. This is the beginning of all the hidden things, which spread out from there and emanate, according to their species. A single point . . . which was concealed, but aroused itself to exist—at first it brought into being a single point, and from there it generated everything" (Matt, *God and the Big Bang*, 41; verb tenses changed).

If science is our human attempt to know, to research and measure and quantify all that we can know, as objectively as we can, religion, our religious awareness of the Oneness of God, brings something else in: *the self* and its yearnings. Religion, awareness of God, asks these questions: Where do I fit in? What is my purpose, my family's purpose, my people's purpose? Religion teaches that those questions have sacred value. Judaism affirms our urge to respond to God, to act, to take responsibility for our lives.

RABBI MAX WEISS

1

I begin with what I know. Knowledge comes from many sources, but what I experience directly is most powerful. I remember when I was a child sitting on the floor with my father. He would take out a flashlight and two balls, one large and one small, and show me how the earth revolved around the sun, how the moon revolved around the earth, how the earth rotated on its axis and how all of those circular motions combined into what we experience as sunrise and sunset, phases of the moon, lunar eclipses, and the gradual transformation of summer heat into winter cold. The simple things I saw, experienced, and lived—the rising and setting of the sun, the waxing and waning of the moon, and the flowing of one season into the next—were all explainable. All were riddles to be solved.

The lesson of those childhood moments was absorbed, and so as I approach God, I must begin with what I have experienced. I first felt God's tangible presence when I was a young teen. Following a day of hiking in the mountains of New Mexico, I rested on a mountain-side, with the browns and greens of a valley stretching to the horizon, and I lost myself. For a time my senses and my self disappeared, and all I felt was oneness, not an interconnectedness of all things, but a unity and sameness of all things. It was a moment of peering beneath the surface, of sensing in the sunset the rotation of the earth. This feeling is experienced across religious traditions and by folks who would claim no religion at all, but in Chasidic tradition it is called *bitul hayeish* (בִּיטּוּל הַיֵּשׁ), nullification of one's somethingness. When experiencing *bitul hayeish*, all sense of self and uniqueness is lost. It is a state incompatible with individual identity. We may sense or experience *bitul hayeish*, but as human beings our bodies place demands on our consciousness, so it is a place we may visit but not a place we may live. That oneness and unity of all is a facet of God. God's proper name *Yod-Hei-Vav-Hei* (יהוה), derived from the Hebrew root that means "to be," is an expression of that unity, of this "is-ness" of all.

When I say the *Sh'ma*, I am saying: Listen Children of Israel, *Yod-Hei-Vav-Hei* is our God, *Yod-Hei-Vav-Hei* is the Unity of all. God does not hide beneath the surface or exist far removed from us. God is the unifying reality of existence.

2

When we speak about evil, we are generally referring to one of two broad categories. The first is evil caused by humans—rape, murder, war, environmental degradation, and so on. The second category of evil is linked to what we would call natural events—hurricanes, earthquakes, childhood diseases, and cancer are among the horrors in this set.

Most attempts to explain evil and its relationship to God explain away evil done by one person to another as being a consequence of free will. Each human being has the ability to choose his or her actions, and some choices are harmful.

The second category of a source of suffering, a natural event, is more difficult to explain in most explorations of God. If God is good, if God knows all, if God is powerful, then why do these naturally occurring horrors happen? The story of the serpent in the Garden of Eden provides some insight, a glimpse beneath the surface of created things. The story in Genesis of the creation of our world is the story of God ordering chaos, turning *tohu vavohu* (תֹהוּ וָבֹהוּ), welter and waste, into water and earth, light and dark, plant and animal, man and woman. But into this ordered structure, the subtle serpent, symbol of the primeval chaos, wormed its way; and from the moment of Creation, the edges of things continually fray.

The ordered universe we inhabit, the totality of all, tends toward chaos. It is the continual outpouring of energy from God that allows order to exist. Suffering and evil in and of themselves serve no God-ordained purpose. They just are.

As expressions of God, it is our human responsibility to work toward an ordered existence; this is the role of mitzvot in Jewish life. Our response to the suffering of others is a recognition of our common humanity and our oneness through God.

3

Mitzvot are the Jewish expression of truths we understand about how God intersects with human life. Mitzvot fit into two broad categories: *mitzvot bein adam LaMakom* (מִצְוֹות בֵּין אָדָם לַמָּקוֹם), those between a person and God, govern our ritual behavior; and *mitzvot bein adam lachaveiro* (מִצְוֹות בֵּין אָדָם לַחֲבֵרוֹ), those between one person and another, govern our interpersonal behavior. Mitzvot can thus speak to every aspect of our lives, just as God exists as every aspect of reality.

An understanding of God that begins with the idea that God is All has profound impact on our ethical behavior. A conviction that all is one leads to a deeply felt empathy for others and motivates us toward deepening our connection to one another and to the universe of which we find ourselves a part.

Key to a sense of universal oneness is a belief in a universal ethic for all humanity. At a base level, this universal ethic is expressed by Rabbi Hillel the Elder, "What is hateful to you, do not do to others" (Babylonian Talmud, *Shabbat* 31a). As a universalization of a human ethic,

Hillel's statement is functional and provides a working structure for the ethics that flow from the idea of a God who encompasses everything. The second and often forgotten half of Rabbi Hillel's statement, "All the rest is commentary, go and study," places his universal ethical value into a particularly Jewish context. If we view all of humanity as equally valuable and worthy and then see all of the rest of Jewish learning and life as support for that unifying belief, as Hillel insists we do, then our ethical values and our Judaism are consistent with a belief in a God that unites all into one.

To ethically live the understanding that all is one and that the One is God means to accept a kinship of all humanity. This has a profound impact on our relationships. For Jews this impact is felt and expressed through mitzvot that show us the way to be in relationship with all others. Using Rabbi Hillel's interpretive lens and imagining ourselves as the other will lead us to interpret *mitzvot bein adam lachaveiro*, mitzvot about our relationships, in a universal light that will link us to the universe that is God.

4

If I believe that I must begin with what I see and experience, then the belief that God is all-good, all-knowing, and all-powerful is impossible for me to hold. History is thick with the unbounded suffering of the innocent. In the time frame of the universe—God's time—human existence barely registers. We are to the cosmos as a molecule of salt is to the ocean, contributing and present but part of a system so large that our existence has only a very local effect. We gain our power, our strength, and our grandeur when we bind ourselves to the immensity of reality.

God enters human history when we bring God into human history. When we act individually and communally according to our ethical mitzvot, we can have a tremendous local effect on our world. Our individual and communal actions can bring us closer to or further from the understanding of unity that is God. Humans are not God, but we exist in God. Nature is not God but exists in God. All that is, is an expression of ineffable totality.

God's role is to be. In God's being is our being, our history, all that is, all that is not yet. Our role, as expressions of God, is to help guide one another into an understanding of our commonality.

RABBI OR ZOHAR

1

My great-grandmother, Mrs. Bertha Levin, may she rest in peace, used to make business with God: "If You will help me put my overshoes on today, I will give such and such money for *tzedakah*." Lately, I have come to appreciate this down-to-earth approach to faith. Similarly, I try to learn from the biblical Abraham and Moses: there was always a great deal of give-and-take and bargaining between them and the Mighty One. In other words: if we are to take Martin Buber's "I-Thou" paradigm seriously, shouldn't our relationship with the Eternal One be as straightforward and unpretentious as this?

So like my ancestors, I seek an intimate relationship with God, and I realize that in this relationship, as in any truly meaningful connection with someone else, I must give in order to receive. I must admit that it is often very difficult. Realizing that to ask God to give me something, I must give Her something in return often makes me lazy and fearful about asking for anything at all. Also, I am often afraid to put my faith to the test, so I tend to procrastinate. In other instances, I actually fake it as I promise God to give up things that I don't really care for in exchange for receiving things that I don't really need.

Fortunately, this vicious cycle of idle miscommunication with myself as well as with my Maker cannot last for eternity, as it often causes unhappiness and frustration. Time and again I am reminded that to develop and transform, I must make a true sacrifice.

In Hebrew, the word for sacrifice is *korban* (קָרְבָּן), which alongside its meaning of "exchanging one thing for another" also means "getting closer to" and also "inward" or "in the guts." This multilayered term assists me in trying to define my theology as a theology of the guts, of seeking intimacy and of offering holy exchange. In other words, my conversation with the Divine tries to include an element of self-examination and an increasing awareness of what my body and soul truly need and desire. It also includes a commitment to try to improve my communication skills in order to create better intimacy with others. It requires making conscientious choices every day, choices that I hope will lead me to "find grace and good favor in the sight of God and people" (Proverbs 3:4).

2

Even though we sometimes tend to blame God for bad things that happen to us, it does not make a lot of sense to do so. It is not a very constructive way to live. Most of the evil and suffering that happens to people is created by people, or at least it could be prevented by them. War and genocide, domestic violence and car accidents, hunger and social injustice, even some fatal diseases—all fall into this major category. I find that blaming God for bad things created by humans is somewhat immature. It is naïve to believe that God is supposed to interfere with our wrongdoings the same way that a teacher intervenes in kindergarten. So one spiritual practice that I try to embrace is that of seeing myself less as God's child and more as God's partner in constantly repairing Creation, as complicated and as imperfect as it may be.

Another important issue in thinking about the question of good and evil is finding the right perspective on things. Many of the things that we categorize as "bad" simply aren't so. Often, it is our ignorance, fear, or lack experience or our inability emotionally to contain certain encounters that creates a sense of suffering that is actually not necessary. It is not uncommon that in retrospect, some incidents or interactions we thought to be terrible actually proved to be a learning experience, however painful, that forced us to grow and develop. Sometimes, it is possible to perceive our enemies and people who do us wrong as messengers of divine providence, who in fact push us toward a positive change we were hesitant to make on our own.

When I try to examine the existence of evil and suffering in this world, I tend to forget that I am often not only the victim, but also the source and perpetrator. In this respect, I think about my relationship with the Divine in terms of truth and awareness (as opposed to self-denial), my ability or inability to forgive myself, take responsibility, create change, and actually become a better person. I tend to agree with those who believe that it is rather difficult to achieve the things mentioned above without the ability to surrender to a higher power—a power that may be revealed within me but is still not me.

3

Quantum physics explains that particles can be both here and there at the same time. Likewise, the mysterious and wonderful thing about God is that She is ever present everywhere and always. This means that somehow we are also divine, and so is everybody else. In my opinion, this basic concept of being created in God's image remains the best paradigm for the development of human ethics. I believe that this paradigm is probably the most fundamental principle in the theology of the Hebrew Bible. This paradigm, however central to our tradition, is far from being perfect and, like many wonderful and great human inventions, needs a serious tool kit to check and ensure its viability.

One of those tools is the dynamic principle. As strange as it might sound to some, religious law must be flexible and ever changing, as is the spiritual experience itself. As we well know, there is a tendency to cast religious rules in stone, and the result is that rules that were just and humane and suitable in certain historical circumstances tend to create injustice and be a source for atrocities once those circumstances change. This is probably why our Sages have taught us that the broken pieces of the tablets are greater than the whole tablets. According to the *Zohar* (*Ra'aya Meheymana*, *Vayikra*, *Parashat Tzav*, 3:27a), this is also the reason why the Torah was given to us by a stutterer, for it remains somewhat ambiguous and is always open for interpretation.

I believe that a central reason for the failure of ethical systems that are based on religion is that they are often based upon the memory of the experience of the past instead of a connection to spiritual inner resources in the present or to a vision for the future. When our spirituality and connection with the Divine is out of tune, so is our morality and our connection to others. As we constantly practice our devotion to God, we discover that the only way to develop spiritually is through our relationships with other beings.

We are sometimes afraid that spiritual experience disconnects us from other people or that it makes us aloof as individuals or racist and particularistic as a community or as a nation. Indeed, this is the case in many instances, but I suggest that whenever this is the case, it is a false spirituality and not a true one. If we follow the quantum-like spiritual paradigm that every divine spark that is revealed within us is also revealed within someone else, certainly this spark must humble us and make us more compassionate toward others.

4

One of the ways that God's presence is revealed in the world is through science. According to the mystical tradition of Kabbalah, God reveals Herself in various ways, one of those ways being our experience of the physical world (for example, see *Zohar*, introduction, 1:1b–2a). In other words, scientific research is holy work, and scientific discovery is the discovery of God's presence in the world. Since our tradition has never read Scripture literally, there is absolutely no need to ponder so-called conflicts between science and faith. Since the Bible consists of myths and metaphors, its holy words should be addressed as such and never as scientific or historical facts.

The only fact that postmodern science assures us of is that the more we know, the more we know that we don't know. In this constant game of hide-and-seek played between us and our Creator, both the concealed and the apparent are divine. Even more so, our curiosity and desire to reveal the secrets of Creation are in themselves a clear emblem of us being created in God's image.

As we can learn from the shape of the punctuation mark representing a question in our culture, each question begins with a point, then goes far out, and finally stretches back toward its original source, without ever actually reaching it, and always coming back from a different angle. This is a wonderful metaphor for thinking about God and science: each scientific question begins with a spark of curiosity that is actually divine. It then sends us out to the world, looking for answers. Once we get the answer, it not only gives us more power and freedom to act in the world, but it also changes who we are. It raises new questions about right and wrong, the use of power, the distribution of natural resources, wealth, and so on.

This is where science, technology, and spirituality meet. Who is asking the questions? Who uses power and to what end? What gives meaning to our endless pursuit after innovations and progress? The answers to those questions lie within the realm of the spiritual: looking back at the point from which the journey began from a different angle, without actually being able to reach it. Like Moses at the gates of the Promised Land, there will always be an unattainable place to reach, another piece missing from the ever-changing puzzle that is divine.

RABBI ELAINE ZECHER

1

My understanding of God is filled with contradictions. How is it possible to turn to the Divine to ask forgiveness—to say *Avinu Malkeinu* when God is neither Father nor King? At the same time, I sense this life force within me that is more than I am and connects me to something larger in the universe. How can it be that when my father died years ago, I derived real comfort in a belief that some essence of him would dwell in God's presence? That presence is everywhere and nowhere, within me, through me, and beyond me; within you, through you, beyond you. No rational explanation applies.

It wasn't until rabbinical school that I began to try to articulate a concept of God. And then I discovered God by discerning the soul. Here's a whopping confession: through all of my intense Jewish involvement in synagogue life and in youth groups growing up in Monroeville, Pennsylvania, no one ever told me I had a soul! I found my soul in rabbinical school. I didn't find it through the assumed way, that is, through a deep and intense engagement with sacred texts, punctuated by meaningful interactions with instructors. I didn't even discover it by presiding over transformative life-cycle rituals and rites in my student pulpit. I found my soul by witnessing the strength and healing power of someone else's soul.

A fellow rabbinical student experienced a terrible accident. She might have died. When I went to see her in the hospital, although she had tubes running in and out of her, she lifted her hand and gave us the thumbs-up, informing us she would be okay and so would we. It was in that moment that I was able to look past her mauled body and see that the marvel of her spirit shone brightly.

Like the soul that we cannot see but gives us life, God, too, is not seen, but is a life-giving and inspiring Force in the universe.

We have access to God and God reaches toward us through our consciousness of God's presence. I have learned that I have to work at experiencing God. In study, in prayer, in meditation, and in acts of loving-kindness, God becomes manifest. The simple act of awareness opens the possibility. The *Zohar* calls God many names and one is *Zot* (זֹאת), "This": this experience in prayer, in study, in relationship, in the quiet moment of vacation or the crazy busy race of the week; in the eyes of a beloved, in the smile of a stranger, in the iridescent orange glow of the setting sun. Then there is no contradiction, really.

2

If theodicy means a defense of God's goodness in view of evil, then we make an assumption that God is connected to evil. The God so many people know comes straight from Bible stories and our initial reactions to them. Without further exploration, that is what remains with us. Isn't God more than that? Many of us reject God not because of a particular image or a specific name, but because other people use the Divine in the name of violence and destruction. Yet, to step away from God because others invoke the divine name in this manner is no excuse. We have the capacity to use our heads along with our hearts to think, ponder, and meditate to discover God's presence in a way that transcends simplified biblical descriptions and manipulation of God's purpose. Too many of us have had to struggle with life's many challenges, both anticipated and unanticipated, yet when there is terrible pain, crisis, or illness, the last thing we would want to exclaim is "This is what God wants!"

God is not in the disease or the tragedy or the evil behavior of some people. God is the realization that this is the unpleasant reality of what we are going through and that this moment is ours to choose how to respond.

The Chasidic master Yaakov Yosef, a student of the Baal Shem Tov, said that the mystery of human beings is that we might be set on the ground but it is possible for our heads to be lifted toward the heavens. On the ground is where we are human, imperfect at best, mortal for sure. Bad things happen. People get sick. People misuse knowledge, power, and money. That's not God. That's us. And yet we can ascend higher toward the metaphorical heavens to pursue justice and goodness and righteousness. God is the alternative to evil and suffering, not because God can make any of it go away, but our own searching and reaching higher can help elevate us in our lives to seek meaning in God's presence in the face of evil and despair.

3

Love cannot be held in the palm of our hand, but we certainly know when it is present. If we are fortunate enough to experience it, we believe in it, seek it, and want to savor it, making sure that our children learn to know it. Describing a flavor like cinnamon to someone else does not adequately explain exactly what the taste of it is. That person has to taste it as well, and his or her experience may be completely different from anyone else's.

The Hebrew word *ladaat* (לָדַעַת), "to know," is associated biblically with a particular intimate act, as in Adam "knew" Eve. But, that same Hebrew word is not used for animals engaged in similar activities. To know is more than a physical act. *Ladaat*—to really know—is the human capacity to demonstrate compassionate awareness in distinguishing another person from other living things.

The pursuit of awareness, of seeking to know God, could easily lead to self-absorption. Too often, the word "spiritual" or its cousin, "spirituality," connotes a religion of Me, and not You. What is the purpose of seeking a higher power if not to sanctify our lives to discover a deeper meaning and purpose for ourselves? If we spend the day in prayer and then walk over the needy and downtrodden, then what we do is in vain, a vain pursuit. Martin Buber suggests that we should start with ourselves but not end with ourselves (*Way of Man*, 31). To what end is this spiritual search if not to end up reaching out to one another? Robert Wright, who penned the *Evolution of God*, traces how people have evolved from primordial ooze into human beings connected in social cohesion and guided by a moral imagination, with God as the compass. For many of us, serving others is the definition of our spiritual selves. And yet in the course of taking care of others, we need not neglect nurturing our inner lives and our awareness of God's presence to sustain us in this sacred work.

4

I try to imagine what the ancients sensed about God. They must have felt a force in the universe, manifest in their world, primarily through nature. The powerful windstorms, the droughts, the magnificence of rebirth each spring must have brought wonder, awe, and a sense of mystery mixed with fear of the unknown and unknowable. They must have had their own questions about the way their world functioned, pondering life and death. Like Adam, the first human who had all the living things paraded in front of him to see what he would call them, the ancients began to name in order to understand what existed. But naming often leads to limiting one's scope, even as it defines, because it creates boundaries. To name God, the ancients used metaphors and images based on human understanding. They equated the likeness of God to the likeness of human beings, which in turn mirrored a likeness of God. It is no wonder that humans like Pharaohs or emperors throughout history would mistake themselves as "gods."

Each act of definition and naming was made in an attempt to understand God, but it moved us a bit further away from having and maintaining a personal relationship with God. God became Other, and we lost that direct sense of mystery, wonder, and fear. Is it possible that in earlier times, our ancestors felt God's presence but lacked the skills to study God and that more recently, we've become skilled at studying God but may have lost the ability to sense God's presence?

Science does not replace mystery. It encourages it. Rational thinking does not negate wonder. It demands cognitive engagement.

The Psalmist, long ago, did not espouse a particular theology to reach God. The Psalmist simply addressed the Divine and allowed the longings of the heart to emerge. Rabbi Abraham Joshua Heschel called the Psalms the birth pangs of theology. Their words can teach us.

The Psalmist said, "This is the day God has made, let us rejoice and be happy in it" (Psalm 118:24). The Psalmist didn't tell us which day. Rashi teaches that each time the word *hayom* (הַיּוֹם), "the day," appears, it is ever present. It is now. This day, this moment, carries God with it if we are willing to be open to be here, mindful of the possibility.

This is what I believe in light of science, history, and nature: our human capacity allows us to call God into our presence simply by our willingness to be fully present and aware.

RABBI JOSH (YOSHI) ZWEIBACK

Dear God,

1

It's been a while since I've written. I know that You understand. (OK—that was presumptuous. I don't really *know* much about You. You are infinite, beyond words, beyond worlds, beyond my finite ability to understand, to know. But my sense—my faith—is that You do understand.) I give thanks to You every day. When I wake, when I eat (although, to be honest, I don't always remember, but I try), when I gather with others to say words of praise and thanks.

But I haven't written, I haven't reached out to You from my heart, from the depths, in a while. It's like that sometimes, our relationship. Sometimes, especially when I'm deep in a forest or high on a mountain or gazing out into the endless expanse of the ocean or the night sky, I feel so close to You. Your presence, the wonder of Your creation, fills me with awe. But other times—now is one of them—You seem distant, detached, wholly Other, transcendent in every way.

I yearn to be close to You but it's hard. It's hard to be in relationship with You—Unseen, Unheard, Mysterious, Transcendent, Hidden . . .

Traces of Your power, of Your Creation, are all around, but too often, I find myself searching for You in vain.

And then—sometimes—comes acceptance and gratitude for all You have done, and the disappointment about our lack of true intimacy slips away.

For this world, O God, I offer You my humble thanks. Life itself is the ultimate gift—You owe us nothing more. You have already given us all we need to live lives of meaning and goodness. In these moments of clarity, I find satisfaction in simply offering You my gratitude for the abundant kindness of Your creation without any expectation of further service to me on Your part.

So, thank You, God, for the universe, for life itself.

2

Having said that, over the years I have had questions for You about all sorts of things in this universe, mainly bad things, that caused me to question You, to doubt You, even to raise my voice in anger or, God forbid, take Your name in vain.

Once, when I was about twelve years old, my parents took me to see the movie *The Elephant Man*. It traumatized me—not the image of his disfigurement, but the cruelty he suffered at the hands of others. I despaired of this world, and I despaired of You. How could You allow it? How could You, God, stand idly by as one of Your creatures was humiliated and tormented, tortured by those whose job it was to protect the most vulnerable?

And later, throughout the years, I asked essentially the same questions about all sorts of things more frightening than the Elephant Man: pogroms and lynchings, gas chambers and killing fields.

Ultimately, I have stopped blaming You for the cruelty and misdeeds of humanity. The capacity for human kindness is considerable. So is its opposite. You have dignified us with the gift of free will—the choice is ours. Will we be kind or will we be cruel? When we fall short, sometimes tragically so, of realizing our potential for goodness, You—I imagine—are disappointed, maybe even disgusted. But You do not intercede. You allow us to make the choices we make and then suffer or enjoy the consequences.

3

I believe, God, that You want us to choose the good but—I'll be honest—it's hard for me sometimes to know what the good choice is. It would be easier if You had provided a clear instruction manual of all of the dos and don'ts. Some would argue that that is what Torah is: the Testament of Your will for humanity. I don't see it that way. For me, Torah is a human document, written over a period of hundreds of years by my ancestors, searching for meaning, searching for answers, searching for truth. Torah is sacred to me because it has been carried by my people for more than three thousand years. It is sacred because my ancestors believed it to be so. It is sacred because—it makes me sad to say this—many of my ancestors died because of their fidelity to it.

But You didn't write it. I don't think You write books. And if You were to write a book, I'd find it strange for You to reveal an unchanging text to just one people, at one time, for a particular context.

This makes things easier and harder for me. It's easier because I don't have to take the narratives of the Torah literally. It's easier because I don't have to pretend that every commandment is an expression of Your ethical perfection. When the Torah commands behavior that I find contrary to the Good, I can—I hope with humility and thoughtfulness—reject that as an error in judgment or logic or even the unfortunate consequence of the historical context in which the author lived. I do not, however, have to try to justify how it is that You, God of Goodness, God of Wisdom, God of Kindness, God who transcends context and gender, could command such a thing.

4

But it makes things harder, too. What is Your will for us? What does it mean for us to behave in accordance with Your will when Your will cannot be known empirically? How are we to behave when two or more values that we believe to be "godly" conflict with one another, when justice and kindness are at odds, when truth and respect bump into one another?

God, I believe that You want us to be good, to be kind, to be fair, to be just, to be loving. I believe that, more than anything, You want us to make the world a better place and, perhaps ultimately, even a perfect place. You have given us everything we need to accomplish this. As nice as a clear instruction manual might be, it would be presumptuous for us to expect this of You.

You owe us nothing because You've already given us everything. Our universe exists because You brought it into being. We exist because You make existence possible.

And so, every day, when I wake, when I eat, when I drink, when I feel—even when I feel lousy—it is my duty to offer You praise and thanks.

So, thank You, God, for everything.

Love,
Yoshi

Section Two

ON OUR HUMANITY

1. What does it mean to be created in the divine image?

2. What does the concept of gender contribute to our understanding of being human?

3. The terms "grace" (חֵן, *chein*), "salvation" (יְשׁוּעָה, *y'shuah*), and "love" (אַהֲבָה, *ahavah*) have been important concepts in Jewish religious vocabulary but are frequently associated with Christianity. What can these terms mean in our contemporary Jewish lives?

4. What is your concept of soul and afterlife?

RABBI LEE BYCEL

1

Traveling through the sub-Saharan desert of Eastern Chad, I saw the boy dressed in rags, standing alone. His sad and hollowed eyes reflected the hopelessness of his situation: a Darfuri refugee living in the midst of dust, disease, and desperation. In my time with the men, women, and children of Darfur, I listened with a broken heart to countless stories of rape, violence, and murder of their loved ones. Yet I will never forget the boy standing there alone.

I returned home with many questions about this boy. *Was this boy created in the divine image?* If so, could I imagine a God overflowing with hurt and desperation clearly being reflected in the image of this sad little boy? I also wondered if the men, the *janjaweed*, who committed atrocities beyond belief against the Darfuri people were created in the divine image. Is there a God that tears people's lives apart, that kills and causes hurts that penetrate so deeply that they can never be healed?

Out in the desert, I considered these questions in a very different way than I ever had from the comfort of my life in the States. The boy (the victim) and the man (the perpetrator) are both created in the divine image. Yet it is nearly impossible to see the Divine in either of them. The divine image reflects goodness, fulfillment, and peace. Where was that to be found in a land of murderous *janjaweed* and innocent victims who now wandered the land in desperation?

Judaism maintains that the human being is created in the divine image. It is often difficult to make out that image amidst the clouds of darkness, death, and destruction that human beings have created. Ultimately, the divine image is in each of us, but it is waiting to be discovered. It is the goodness that resides in each of us. It is that "still small voice" of conscience that pleads with us to look for the sacred in other human beings and implores us to treat other people with dignity, which includes making sure that all human beings have food, water, and shelter as well as opportunities to live a sacred life. It is that innate instinct that drives us to create and not to destroy, to lift up and not to tear down. The divine image is peace incarnate, our instinct to pursue peace in each and every place that human beings interact with each other. The divine image is that uniquely human potentiality for affirming that which is good. It is our inner compulsion to choose life.

2

Sitting in tents of the Darfuri refugees and hearing their plight, I asked myself: What is it to be fully human? This, I believe, is the most challenging question that we face. We seem to spend a lot of time on theological questions: Is there a God? How can God allow human beings to suffer? Do I believe in God? Although worth examining, I believe that throughout the ages, we have devoted an excess of time to questions about God and far too little time to questions about the human condition. We are infants in our understanding of what it means to be human. I often wonder whether humanity has progressed much from the story of the first two brothers, Cain brutally killing Abel.

Gender is one important factor that enriches our understanding of what it is to be human. Men's primitive forebears were hunters and predators; and from the beginning of time, men have been the perpetrators of most of the violence, destruction, and genocide that has been done to other human beings. It is men who have shaped a construct of life that is violent and destructive.

Men living in the twenty-first century must begin to confront this history and reflect carefully on their own individual behavior. Although most men have not committed horrific acts against women, men should be asking if they have done enough to create a world wherein violence aimed at women is no longer tolerated. Today, men must strive to develop more compassion, kindness, and love toward women. They must also learn to resist the temptation to dominate others.

Historically, women have been the victims of war, rape, and abuse. It is women who have seen their worlds torn apart by the cruelty of men. It is women who have held home and community together. It is women who have found wellsprings of forgiveness and compassion in their hearts.

Women living in the twenty-first century must continue to explore their own history. It is critical that they remain resolutely committed to living lives that do not emulate the worst qualities of men but rather uplift the humane parts of women and men.

It was Abraham Joshua Heschel who challenged both men and women to ask themselves an entirely different question. Heschel wrote, "We ask: What is man? Yet the true question should be: Who is man?" (Heschel, *Who Is Man?*, 28; Heschel died in 1972, and it is clear in his work that "man" refers to both men and women).

When we ask "Who is man?" instead of "What is man?" we commit ourselves to exploring all of our qualities as human beings, including gender. How do I kindle the humanness inside of me and others? What is it to be human and humane? Can we change the human condition?

3

As I sat with a teenage Darfuri girl who told me her story of being raped, I wondered where were grace, salvation, and love in her life;

where are those ideals in the lives of victims throughout the world? These concepts, which are taken seriously by Christians, are often neglected by Jews. As a result of my travels in the world of the dispossessed in Darfur, I have come to better understand the Jewish notions of grace, salvation, and love. For the contemporary Jew, these concepts need to be reclaimed.

Salvation is about doing what we can to help or save others from harm. For Jews, divine salvation comes through our efforts to advance the salvation of our fellow human beings. The measure of our lives is found in what we do to help people who are hurting. We find salvation in creating ways for the powerless and the victims of the storms of life "to be helped" by changes in society that allow them to be active participants in redeeming their dignity and their lives.

Similarly, grace in Judaism comes through the way we live our lives. Those who live in a humble manner and show loving-kindness toward others may be said to have grace. It often appears that we human beings have lost a sense of graciousness that also includes gratitude. Love is a core human need. Who does not wish to be loved or to find a way to love? Love is an art that needs to be nurtured. It requires both a striving to avoid harsh judgments of others and finding ways to support and love the vulnerable and the dispossessed, those who are in such desperate need of love and support.

In *Pirkei Avot* we are taught, "If I am not for myself, who will be for me? If I am only for myself, what am I? If not now, when?" (*Pirkei Avot* 1:14). From this insightful teaching we learn that all life is a daily search for the equilibrium that keeps love of self and love of others in proper balance. So it is with the ideals of grace, love, and salvation. If I am not kind to myself, if I do not love myself, and if I do not protect myself, who will do these things for me? Yet if I am not kind to others, if I do not love my brothers and sisters, and if I do not protect them, what am I? If I do not start to live a life filled with the qualities of grace, love, and salvation now, when will I ever start? Jewish teachings prompt us to search for the delicate balance that falls between the antipodes of selfishness and selflessness. This search is a lifelong journey.

4

For the ancient Greeks, the human soul distinguished us from animals and reflected our ability to reason. In Judaism, the soul has been perceived as the quality that enables us to see the sacred in others and in ourselves. The soul is not a material object, and it cannot be dissected and studied; yet it is as real any as any physical part of our selves. One cannot experience the soul through the five physical senses, yet the soul can indeed be apprehended through our spiritual senses.

It is in the soul that one has a profound emotional appreciation of the natural world—the spectacular beauty of a sunset or a sunrise. It is in the soul that one can appreciate inner beauty in other human beings. One who has a mature soul has a deep appreciation of the plight of all human beings and their yearnings and hopes.

Our concern should be the nurturing and enhancing of the soul. This can be achieved when we look for the transcendent experiences in life—through the beauty that we find in nature, in the arts, in music, in prayer, and in any other activity that moves us emotionally. In this way, we develop a heightened sense of our own humanity as well as the humanity of others.

The afterlife is unknown and often is the source of great anxiety and fear. This is understandable, as this is how we face life—spending so much of life resisting change and afraid of what we do not know. The unknown in life has become a source of terror rather than a source of prospect and hope. We often shelter ourselves from facing that which pushes us out of our comfort zone and into an area of discomfort. The Jewish journey through life is one that embraces change and growth and provides us with a road map for exploring the unknown as we go through the various stages of life.

I believe there is an afterlife. Yet I am also convinced that this afterlife is unimaginable and unknowable. I prefer to think about this unknown stage that awaits all human beings as a time of prospect and hope. We best prepare for the afterlife by learning how to embrace the unknown in life and believing that no matter how dark the night, light will come in the morning. In other words, we learn how to understand the afterlife through our present life. We do this when we see that hopeless boy in the desert of Darfur and, despite all odds, we choose to act on our belief that one distant day this same boy will yet live with dignity, purpose, and hope.

RABBI MICAH CITRIN

1

Too often we worry about our inclination to anthropomorphize God. But perhaps we have it wrong. It is not God who has human characteristics, but we who have godly characteristics. We are a dim reflection of the Creator here on earth, "little less than divine," as the Psalmist suggests (Psalm 8:6). We possess transcendent, holy attributes even as we are limited by mortality and the flaws each of us struggles to subdue, accept, and overcome during the course of our lifetime.

A fundamental source of our divine reflection radiates from one of the few dogmas Jews embrace about God: *Sh'ma Yisrael, Adonai Eloheinu, Adonai Echad* (שְׁמַע יִשְׂרָאֵל יְהוָה אֱלֹהֵינוּ יְהוָה אֶחָד), "Hear O, Israel, *Adonai* is our God, *Adonai Echad.*" When we declare God *Echad*, One, it goes beyond a statement of quantity, that there is only One God. We cannot quantify the Infinite. Rather, *Echad* means wholly unique, holy in otherness and distinction, complete in unity. God is the complete Oneness that pervades existence, singular in being, whose essence is quality, not quantity.

Like God, each of us is unique, a singular being. Even though we are born from our parents and carry the traits of our family gene pool, we each exist as a unique manifestation of life. The Talmud illustrates this divine gift in a story that seeks to explain the distinctive nature of each person.

Adam, the first human, was created alone, according to the Rabbis, in order to proclaim the greatness of God. The story continues, "Our Rabbis taught that if a person mints coins from the same mold, they all turn out alike. Yet, God fashioned each human being from the same mold, Adam, but not one person is alike" (Babylonian Talmud, *Sanhedrin* 38a).

More than just the stamp of a common humanity, we are stamped with the image of God. Every human being shares this commonality, yet in God's image we are each unique, completely different from anyone who has ever lived or who ever will live. We each exist as one of a kind, experiencing God's world, and contributing to it, in our own way. This is God's promise to us, the spark of the Holy One within us, and it lends us the overwhelming sense of the precious nature of our lives. Humanity becomes the vessel through which *Echad* is projected into this world. Our task is to live with this awareness and conduct ourselves in a manner that is worthy of this image.

2

Genesis chapters 1 and 2 present instructive lenses for how we might understand the influence of gender on our humanity. Genesis 1:27 narrates the creation of the human being, "And God created Adam in God's image; in God's image, God created Adam—male and female—God created them." From this text we learn that the human being, *male and female*, is created in the likeness of God. In her book *God and the Rhetoric of Sexuality*, Phyllis Trible asserts that *Adam* is not one creature that is both male and female, but two creatures, one male and one female. She continues, "*Ha-Adam* is not an original unity split apart by sexual division. Instead, it is the original unity that is at the same time the original differentiation" (Trible, *God and the Rhetoric of Sexuality*, 18). In this story, man and woman are equal in origin even as they are distinct sexes. Insofar as both are created in God's image, male and female exist within the transcendence of God. Here on earth, male and female cannot exist as a unity or single entity, but both play a role in completing humanity through their difference and, ideally, through their equality.

Genesis 2 offers a different legacy regarding gender. In this familiar story, *HaAdam*, a male, is created first out of the earth. To remedy Adam's loneliness, God creates a woman Eve out of Adam's rib. Upon seeing Eve, Adam declares, "This time— / bone of my bone, flesh of my flesh! / Let this one be called woman, / for this one is taken from man" (Genesis 2:23). This story sets up an unequal dynamic as man precedes woman, and woman appears to be merely an extension of man. We can see how this text has been used through history to reinforce a hierarchy of man over woman and perpetuate a construct in which male is normal while female is a facsimile of the original. This text suggests an inherent essence to maleness and femaleness, yet we must be aware that society and culture construct the definition of gender.

Genesis 1 points us toward an ideal that recognizes male and female as manifestations of the Source of All Life. Thus, both male and female are necessary to realize a perfected world. Genesis 2 reminds us that this ideal has not yet been achieved because much of human history chronicles the subjugation of women based on human designations of what men and women are or should be. Both men and women have suffered as a result of these constructs. These texts can guide us to heal this broken part of our humanity.

3

Grace, salvation, and love comprise profound religious experiences. Engaging these concepts through a lens of Hebrew can help us to become more comfortable with them as Jews.

Chein, grace, is what we experience in life in spite of ourselves, regardless of what we might deserve. On Rosh HaShanah and Yom

Kippur we call out to God, *Avinu Malkeinu* ***choneinu*** *vaaneinu ki ein banu maasim*—(אָבִינוּ מַלְכֵּנוּ חָנֵּנוּ וַעֲנֵנוּ כִּי אֵין בָּנוּ מַעֲשִׂים)—*Avinu Malkeinu* show us **grace** and answer us though we have done little to deserve it. I feel a sense of *chein* in the renewal of the New Year, being forgiven by loved ones, and receiving a second chance. I also feel *chein* when I eat. In *Birkat HaMazon*, the blessing following a meal, we say, *Hazan et haolam kulo b'tuvo,* ***b'chein,*** *b'chesed, uv'rachamim* (הַזָּן אֶת־הָעוֹלָם כֻּלּוֹ בְּטוּבוֹ, בְּחֵן בְּחֶסֶד וּבְרַחֲמִים)—Blessed are You, God, who gives sustenance to the whole world with goodness, **grace**, compassion, and mercy. There is nothing that we as individuals have done to merit this goodness of eating other than being one of God's creatures. *Chein* fills me with a sense of humility and gratitude.

The twentieth-century philosopher Rabbi Mordecai Kaplan described God as "the power that makes for salvation" (Kaplan, "What Is Our Human Destiny?" 99). For Kaplan, *y'shuah* (יְשׁוּעָה) "salvation" is the potential that exists in the world to overcome and transcend. We find *y'shuah* at the heart of the Exodus story. Trapped between an advancing Egyptian army and the Sea of Reeds, the Israelites are in narrow straits. Moses encourages the Israelites, "Have no fear! Stand by, and witness the *y'shuah* (salvation) of *Adonai*" (Exodus 14:13). *Y'shuah* enables me to find stable footing when I face my own personal Egypt and when I confront the sea of life that at times can be overwhelming. As the prophet Isaiah proclaims, *U'shavtem mayim b'sason mimaay'nei* ***hay'shuah*** (וּשְׁאַבְתֶּם מַיִם בְּשָׂשׂוֹן מִמַּעַיְנֵי הַיְשׁוּעָה)—Joyfully draw water from the wells of salvation (Isaiah 12:3). *Y'shuah* resides in cisterns of spiritual strength we draw from within, from Torah, and from community. It is replenished by the limitless Power That Makes for Salvation all around us.

Two commandments serve as bookends for the ideal of love in the Jewish tradition. At one end we find *V'ahavta et Adonai Elohecha* (וְאָהַבְתָּ אֵת יְהוָה אֱלֹהֶיךָ)—You shall love *Adonai* your God (Deuteronomy 6:5), and on the other end, *V'ahavta l'rei-acha kamocha* (וְאָהַבְתָּ לְרֵעֲךָ כָּמוֹךָ)—

Love your fellow as yourself (Leviticus 19:18). *Ahavah* (אַהֲבָה) calls us to embrace the Source of All Life. We achieve this by looking into the faces of our fellow human beings and recognizing a spark of the Divine looking back at us. This should evoke compassion in our hearts. The singer/songwriter Paul Simon observes in one of his songs, "You ask somebody to love you, you've got a lot of nerve" ("Look at That," from the album *You're the One*). I sometimes wonder: What makes me worthy of love? Perhaps this too is an act of grace. My response to the love I feel from my parents, my children, my wife, my friends, and God is not only to love them back, but also to love the stranger as my personal contribution of *ahavah* to the world.

4

One of my favorite nineteenth- to twentieth-century Zionist thinkers Micha Yosef Berdichevsky, an avowed secularist, wrote one of the most deeply religious reflections that I know. "All things pray," he wrote, "and all things exhale their souls. . . . Creation is itself but a sweetness and a longing, a sort of prayer to the Almighty" (Berdichevsky, *Meditations*, 318). If all creations "exhale their souls," and there is longing built into the very fabric of life, then there must be a Soul of the Universe who implants this soul into all living things. The very name of God in the Jewish tradition that we cannot pronounce, *Yod-Hei-Vav-Hei* (יהוה), comes from the Hebrew verb "to be." God is "Being" whose Infinite *n'shimah* (נְשִׁימָה), "breath," becomes our *n'shamah* (נְשָׁמָה), "soul." And though this *n'shimah* animates all life, it is the human *n'shamah* that is unique. Our soul matches the Soul of the Universe in consciousness. We are aware of the pulsing of life in our bodies, hearts, and minds and of our own longing during our precious, yet brief existence.

I am not sure if there is a heaven or a world-to-come. This is a difficult theology for me to fathom, yet I have abiding faith in the immortality of the soul. In physics we learn that matter can be neither created nor destroyed. I believe that the same is true of our souls. Once it is breathed into us by God, our *n'shamah* never ceases to exist. Our soul, that seed of consciousness, returns to the Soul of the Universe when our bodies die. It is sustained in the memories of those who survive us, and even when we cease to be remembered our soul remains. Our souls are the residue of God entrusted to us in life, our *tzelem Elohim*, or image of God, from which we exist. Just as each of us is unique in time and space, our souls are immutable even as they return to the eternal rhythm of life's respiration.

I am heartened when I pray these words from the morning liturgy: "O God, the soul that You have given me is pure." Yet, with this awareness I also know that the quality of my actions has the power to either taint or elevate my soul. And so when I lie down to sleep and whisper these words with yearning, *B'yado afkid ruchi* (בְּיָדוֹ אַפְקִיד רוּחִי)—In Your hand I place my spirit, I pray that my soul might be worthy of its Source in life and that one day it will share in eternity after my death.

RABBI BENJAMIN DAVID

1

A few years ago, a bat mitzvah student of mine built a playground. She gathered her friends, raised the money, obtained the necessary permits, and made real the idea of a glowing new playground in a New York neighborhood badly in need of one. This became a significant component of her bat mitzvah experience and a reminder to her that to become an adult in the Jewish community is to think deeply about what it means to be there for others. That she chose to give of her energy and artistic talents in the name of children who do not have access to clean, safe environments for play keeps alive a tradition of *tikkun olam* dating back to the Torah itself. From Abraham offering shelter to three passersby to his later seeking out a sanctified burial ground for his beloved wife, we see once and again that to be a Jew is to recognize that like God, we have the capacity to bring great good and great kindness to our world.

The building of a playground reminds us that as human beings, we have the power to build not only important things, but lasting relationships. Not only did she help construct the swings and slides, but she also connected in profound ways with the children who would enjoy these elements for years to come. She came to realize, as we all must strive to remember, that each one of us was created in the divine image. Therefore, like God, we can bring to this world sanctuaries large and small, from soaring religious spaces to much-needed classrooms, treatment centers, shelters, medical marvels, sites for innovation and research, and libraries. And, like God, we can develop relationships that lift us up, give us the strength to carry on, and lend the perspective we so need, for just as God created our awesome and mysterious world in six dramatic days, God spent the rest of the Torah, and beyond, fostering deep relationships with humanity.

To be created in the divine image is to be empowered. To be created in the divine image is to know that in your hands is great power: power to enact change, power to heal, power to grant compassion and strength. From greeting the stranger to being there for the bereaved, to be created in the divine image is to know that God is with and within you, as God was with so many before you, your grandparents and mine, our biblical ancestors, the iconic leaders of Israel, and the countless figures that connect us to the very beginning of the Book of *B'reisheit* (Genesis). This is a message that resonates for all of us, not just those wide-eyed bar and bat mitzvah students preparing to take on adult Jewish life.

2

My understanding of gender in Judaism is no doubt informed by the unique and rich relationships I have shared with multiple male teachers I have known. From my grandfather to my father, to many of the male rabbis I have known throughout my life, I have come to see what it means to be an upstanding Jewish male in today's world. Just as my wife draws inspiration from Rebekah and Rachel, Ruth and Deborah, so do I draw inspiration from Noah, Jacob, Nachshon, and so many others.

What does it mean to be a Jewish male? It means that I find myself at the end of a long line of figures who, like me, lived with a blend of faith and doubt, wisdom and uncertainty, direction and wandering. Jacob wrestled with God above, a God that seemed at times so foreign and unknowable and at times so very close. Jonah grappled with what it meant to be both singular and very much part of a broader Jewish community. These are the traditions I inherit, the role models I turn to as I traverse today's wilderness.

So many of the figures who appear in our canon of stories were defined in large part by their gender. That they were sons and brothers, husbands and fathers, mattered greatly and played a significant role in who they were, how they viewed themselves, and what they were always in the process of becoming as Jews. Isaac was a questioning son. Joseph was a beleaguered brother. As a group, the patriarchs show us Judaism's definition of manhood. They give Jewish men of our own era the permission to be only the best version of themselves, and not the over-idealized, fabricated version of perfection that modern-day society and popular entertainment perpetuate. To be a Jewish man in various ways is to counteract those hardened popular depictions in the name of a more caring, more present, and far more giving existence.

3

The Talmud equates grace with fear of God, as Rabbi Chama bar Papa notes: "The grace of the Eternal is from everlasting to everlasting upon they that fear the Eternal" (Babylonian Talmud, *Sukkah* 49b; quoting Psalm 103:17). This juxtaposition of fear and grace is incredibly apt, especially today.

We live in a time in which fear is justified. We are fearful as parents, as children, as Jews, and no doubt as citizens of an increasingly volatile world. In the most ironic of ways, the fear we feel most is the fear of our fellow human beings. I stood in Lower Manhattan as humans maliciously guided two planes into the Twin Towers. I saw the searing pain that comes with loss. I saw fear with my own eyes and felt fear pulsing in my own veins. A decade later, I crossed the finish line of the Boston Marathon, only to see once more the fear that comes as a result of horrid acts of terror. Those murderous moments, which changed the lives of so many, moments of such suffering brought on by human beings, embody fear.

In both instances, we learned anew that to be human is to live with the ability to choose, and thus to be able to move daily in the direction of either great hurt or great healing. This is the juxtaposition we consider as we hold our hand to the braided candle during *Havdalah*. Will I pursue a week of light or darkness? This is the juxtaposition we refer to on Yom Kippur as our Torah portion of *N'tzavim* urges us to "choose life—if you and your offspring would live" (Deuteronomy 30:19). Will I pursue a year of kindness or enmity?

It is precisely because we are so acquainted with fear that we also know that grace and certainly love are real and are as necessary as ever. Just as the braided candle can cloak the hand in shadows, so can it show us the light that our hands can bring to this world so in need of light. In the days following September 11, 2001, and the days following the bombings at the Boston Marathon in 2013, even more than we saw fear, we saw love. We saw light. We saw community, a coming together of men and women, young and old, in the name of mending and in the name of an eternally bound human family. We realized once more that we find God in those moments of togetherness, those sacred exchanges of support and help. God was in the outpouring of scholarships and donations. With the atrocities of 9/11 and Newtown, Connecticut, and Boston, Massachusetts, still fresh in our minds, God could be found in the willingness to put the needs of the bereaved before every other need. God was in our very ability to still believe in the idea of a good and benevolent God above, the very idea of grace and love, and the unflagging idea of hope.

4

Reform Judaism teaches that while "the dust returns to the earth, the spirit returns to God who gave it." It is only the "house of the spirit" that is placed in the grave (Polish, *Rabbi's Manual*, 159). What is this spirit? What, after all, is a soul? The Hebrew word is *n'shamah* (נְשָׁמָה), which comes from the same root as the Hebrew word for "breath," or *n'shimah*. The idea, perhaps, is that the souls of our departed loved ones live on in our very breath. They survive in our reminiscing of the times shared. They survive in the stories we continue to tell with heavy hearts and slow-moving tears. They survive in the tender invocation of their names at our celebrations and milestones.

We might ask what connects the three consecutive Torah portions in Leviticus of *Acharei Mot*, *K'doshim*, and *Emor*. On the surface they are three very different portions. Perhaps they exist to remind us that (to translate each of their titles) "after death" there is "holiness" in what is "said." This is to say that we further consecrate those human beings who have touched our lives when we remember them for the good and we speak their name in tribute. When we name our children for our own grandparents. When we give *tzedakah* in the name of those we have lost. When we quietly recite the Mourner's *Kaddish* while standing amidst a supportive community. In all of these ways, we are reminded that the soul, the *n'shamah*, survives eternally and that God has indeed implanted eternal life within every one of us.

RABBI DENISE EGER

1

> Rabbi Akiva would say, "Beloved is humanity for we were made in the image of God. And doubly beloved are we for God made it known to us that we are made in God's image."
>
> —*Pirkei Avot* 3:14

Judaism teaches that humanity was created in the image of God. This principle, known in Hebrew as *b'tzelem Elohim* (בְּצֶלֶם אֱלֹהִים), comes directly from the Torah. In Genesis 1:26–27 the text tells us:

> God now said, "Let us make human beings in Our image, after Our likeness; and let them hold sway over the fish of the sea and the birds of the sky, over the beasts, over all the earth, over all that creeps upon the earth." So God created the human beings in [the divine] image, creating [them] in the image of God, creating them male and female.

This is a most profound statement. Human beings are godlike. Not gods themselves, but fashioned after the image of God. We know what human beings look like, but what does God look like? Are we to infer that God has limbs and a face? Or is there something else being taught by these passages?

Our rabbis and our teachers rejected the idea of the physical resemblance between humankind and God. In fact, God rejects this as well in the Ten Commandments: we are told, "Make no graven images" (Exodus 20:4). We are not to represent God in any physical form, not with carvings, drawings, or idols so prevalent in our worlds, both ancient and contemporary. But our rabbis and sages did teach that human beings can strive to have god-like qualities. They base this on a passage in our Torah, "You shall be holy, for I, the Eternal your God, am holy" (Leviticus 19:2).

Judaism has embraced this ideal of a God we cannot see but a God we can feel and come to know through our study of Torah, through our performance of our sacred responsibilities—a God who has a relationship with the community of Israel and the world. God is found in the way we fulfill the mitzvot. So as we "Remember the Sabbath day and keep it holy" (Exodus 20:8) or obey "You must have completely honest weights and completely honest measures" (Deuteronomy 25:15), we are striving to live in the image of God.

This story from the Talmud frames the meaning of *b'tzelem Elohim*, being made in the image of God:

> Rabbi Chama, son of Rabbi Chanina, said: What does the Torah mean when it says, "You shall walk in the ways of *Adonai*" (Deuteronomy 13:5)? Can a person really walk in the shadow of the Divine Presence? Rather, it means that you should imitate the ways of God. Just as God clothed the naked (as it says: "And God made garments of skin for Adam and his wife and clothed them" [Genesis 3:21]), so you shall clothe the naked. Just as God visited the sick ("And God appeared before Abraham" [after his circumcision] [Genesis 18:1]), so you should visit the sick; just as God buried the dead (as it says: "And God buried Moses in the valley" [Deuteronomy 34:6]), so you should bury the dead; and just as God comforts the grieving (as it says: "After the death of

> Abraham, God blessed Isaac his son" [Genesis 25:11]), so you too should comfort the grieving. (Babylonian Talmud, *Sotah* 14a)

The meaning of *b'tzelem Elohim* means striving to live a life of fairness, justice, compassion, understanding, and holiness. These are the attributes of the Divine One that humanity can live by.

2

"So God created the human beings in [the divine] image, creating [them] in the image of God, creating them male and female" (Genesis 1:27). The biblical view of gender is a binary one. God made men, and God made women. Genesis is telling us that there are two sexes. Sex is the physical attributes of the male body and female body and contributes to defining the gender of a person. Jewish tradition has strictly defined sex roles for men and women. Men are halachically (legally) responsible for certain mitzvot and women for other mitzvot, even as women are prohibited from performing some religious obligations. So figuring out who is male and female is important in traditional Judaism.

But gender is not just about genitalia. It is also about different structures, hormones, and some evidence that the brain is wired differently in men and in women. Gender is also about expression of self and our internal perceptions of ourselves, as well as the roles and behaviors we express in the world. Combined, this is how we view ourselves and other human beings in the world.

The truth is that there are many variations of gender identity.

Simply dividing human beings into two categories is not sufficient. Even the Rabbis understood that God created a whole rainbow of humanity. Later Rabbinic texts recognized at least six genders, according to Rabbi Eliot Kukla ("Terms for Gender Diversity in Classical Jewish Texts"): *zachar* (זָכָר, male); *n'keivah* (נְקֵבָה, female); *androgynos* (אַנְדְּרוֹגִינוֹס), a person who has both male and female genitalia;

tumtum (טוּמְטוּם), a person whose genitalia are hidden or obscured; *aylonit* (אַיְלוֹנִית), a person who is identified as "female" at birth but develops "male" characteristics at puberty and is infertile; and *saris* (סָרִיס), a person who is identified as "male" at birth but develops "female" characteristics at puberty and/or is lacking a penis (this can happen naturally or as a result of castration).

Gender informs our view of the world and our experience of the world. Gender is filtered through both the physical body (our sex) and the way others educate and see us in the world.

In Reform Judaism, we recognize the variety of human experiences, and our theology reflects the variety of human beings as a normal and healthy expression of humanity. Reform Judaism, based on an egalitarian approach to women's and men's religious obligations, ought to also embrace the varieties of human gender expression and strive to welcome all under the covenant of Abraham and Sarah.

3

The terms "grace" (*chein*, חֵן), "salvation" (*y'shuah*, יְשׁוּעָה), and "love" (*ahavah*, אַהֲבָה) have been important concepts in Jewish religious vocabulary but are frequently associated with Christianity. What can these terms mean in our contemporary Jewish lives?

Christian apologetics have often usurped Jewish religious categories for their own purposes by redefining Christianity as a religion of love while reframing Judaism as a religion of harsh judgment. This was a tactic to gain followers among the pagans/gentiles of the world once Paul opened the doors to them. This helped the early Church fathers gain traction by painting Christianity as a successor religion to Judaism.

The ideals of grace, salvation, and love, however, are woven throughout our Jewish heritage. God's grace and love cause the gift of Torah to be revealed to the people Israel. The covenant given to our ancestors, Abraham, Isaac, and Jacob, Sarah, Rebekah, Rachel, and Leah, was expanded by Torah through God's grace and love for the people Israel. As our prayers say, "God, remember the good deeds of our ancestors."

At Sinai the people accepted the Torah with the words *Naaseh v'nishma* (נַעֲשֶׂה וְנִשְׁמָע)—We will do and we will observe (Exodus 24:7). Israel's loving reply affirms God's gracious gift, thereby bearing witness to God's grace and love. All we have belongs to God, and we are grateful for the opportunity to grow and receive the blessings of grace and love from the Holy One of Blessing.

That bond of love between Israel and God is expressed throughout the Torah by the idea of our eternal covenant. Even when Israel strays from the path of the covenant or forgets that "the earth belongs to God and its fullness thereof, the world and they that dwell therein" (Psalm 24:1), the covenant can be renewed through the practice of *t'shuvah* (תְּשׁוּבָה). Repentance allows for salvation, helping us to draw near to God once again. When we sin, when we have strayed from our Jewish traditions and responsibilities (mitzvot), we can return to God and to our highest selves through repentance, prayer, and charitable acts. Humanity is not evil at its core, according to Jewish teachings. Rather, human beings have free will to choose blessing or curse, life or death. By love and grace, we hope God will accept our prayer and our repentance.

Salvation occurs when, with God's help, we restore our lives to wholeness and completeness.

Salvation is not some outer event or an experience to be realized only in death; rather, salvation comes through God's grace and love and blessings. Our return and drawing near to God ought to increase our sense of peace and wholeness. We draw near through acts of loving-kindness, prayer, *tzedakah*, and the study of Torah.

4

I believe in the eternity of the soul. Each day we give thanks not only for the body God gives us but also for our *n'shamah* (נְשָׁמָה), our soul, which is the breath of God that lives within each person. The Book of Genesis teaches us, "Then *Adonai*, God, fashioned the man—dust from the soil—and breathed into his nostrils the breath of life, so that the man became a living being" (2:7). God ensouled the first human being, Adam, with the divine breath. We have a bit of eternity and divinity inside of us. The prayer *Elohai N'shamah* (אֱלֹהַי נְשָׁמָה) focuses on our breath as the essence of our soul. Our soul is the essence of our inner being.

Jewish tradition strives to teach us to become better human beings, to walk in God's ways. The prophet Micah teaches us this: "What does God require of you? Only to do justice, love compassion, and walk humbly with your God" (Micah 6:8). These are not mere exhortations. The teaching of our Torah is training for the soul's elevation. Yearning to be one with God or to cling to God recalls a time when our souls were one with the Source we call God.

Thus our acts of justice and compassion, as well as our emphasis on study, *talmud Torah* (תַּלְמוּד תּוֹרָה), are ways to perfect our intellect and our souls. Souls strive for a higher plane, and our system of mitzvot helps us work toward that goal. Our souls are reaching higher and higher, evolving the more we study Torah and the more acts of kindness we perform in the world.

When we die, our body stops, but our soul, our mass of energy, does not die. It returns to the Spirit of the universe, the Energy that we call God, the Intellect we call God, and is absorbed and reunited. The folk custom of opening a window or door when in a room where someone dies is to let the soul fly free to return to God, who gave it. The soul does not remain trapped in the body. The life force of humanity, the soul, is eternal.

RABBI STEPHEN LEWIS FUCHS

1

Being created in God's image certainly does not mean that we look like God. It means that of all the creatures on earth, we have the most godlike powers. It means that we human beings are in charge of and responsible for life on this planet. It is an awesome responsibility with which God has entrusted us.

God charges us in Genesis 1:28:

> פְּרוּ וּרְבוּ וּמִלְאוּ אֶת הָאָרֶץ וְכִבְשֻׁהָ וּרְדוּ בִּדְגַת הַיָּם וּבְעוֹף הַשָּׁמַיִם
> וּבְכָל חַיָּה הָרֹמֶשֶׂת עַל הָאָרֶץ.
>
> *P'ru urvu u'milu et haaretz v'chibshuha urdu bidgat hayam uv'of hashamayim uv'chol chaya haromeset al haaretz.*

My rendering of this passage is: "Be fruitful and multiply and fill up the earth and take responsibility for it. And rule compassionately over the fish of the sea, the birds of the air, and all the living things that creep on the earth."

My translation reflects the midrashic teaching (*B'reishit Rabbah* 8:11) that we human beings stand midway between God and all the other animals on earth. Like the animals, we eat, drink, sleep, eliminate our wastes, procreate, and die. But in a godlike way, we have the power to think, analyze, communicate, and shape our environment in a manner far beyond other creatures.

In the afternoon service for Yom Kippur in *Gates of Repentance* (415) we find a magnificent liturgical expression of what it means to be created in the divine image:

> We were unlike other creatures.
> Not for us the tiger's claws,
> the elephant's thick hide,
> or the crocodile's scaly armor.
> To the gazelle we were slow of foot,
> to the lioness a weakling,
> and the eagle thought us bound to earth.
> But You gave us powers they could not comprehend:
> a skillful hand,
> a probing mind . . .
> a soul aspiring to know and fulfill its destiny.

Being created in the divine image means that we humans are the only creatures on earth who can mine iron ore from the side of a mountain and turn the iron into steel. From that steel, we forge the most delicate of instruments with which to operate on a human brain or an open heart, or we use that steel to make weapons whose only purpose is to kill and maim. Being created in God's image means we have awesome, earth-enhancing, or earth-shattering power.

God's hope in creating us in the divine image is that we use our power to help create on this planet a more just, caring, and compassionate society than exists today. But we—not God—will decide if we choose to do so or not.

2

Ever since I wrote my rabbinical thesis "The Expansion of Women's Rights during the Period of the Mishnah," I have been aware of the extraordinary lengths the Rabbis went to enhance the status of women in Jewish law. The *ketubah*, the Jewish marriage contract, provided economic security for the woman—unprecedented in human history—when the marriage ended through divorce or the husband's death. It is hard to find a more significant advancement in women's rights in legal history.

The Sages de facto eliminated the biblical procedure of *sotah* (Numbers 5:11–31) and the binding of a widow to her brother in-law by levirate marriage against her will (Deuteronomy 25:1–10). Although only the man can divorce the woman—not the other way around—in traditional Jewish law, the Rabbis instituted important procedures whereby if the man did not live up to the provisions of the *ketubah*, she could take him to court and force him to divorce her and pay the face value of the contract.

Over and over again in the Bible it is the woman who demonstrates practical, moral, and spiritual insight. Eve is the heroine of the elevation of humanity. It was she, not her husband, who perceived that life in Eden—while idyllic—was sterile and essentially without meaning. It was she who saw *v'nechmad ha-eitz l'haskil* (וְנֶחְמָד הָעֵץ לְהַשְׂכִּיל), "how desirable the insight was that the tree would bring; she took some of its fruit and ate" (Genesis 3:6). Other examples abound: Rebekah, Esther, Ruth, Deborah, Yael—all visionaries and activists.

The task of our generation is twofold: (1) to interpret the Bible to all of those who will hear our voices and/or read our words to give women the enormous credit they are due but do not receive in traditional circles, and (2) to continue the forward progress in women's rights begun by the Sages of the Mishnah until women and men are held in completely equal regard.

3

For me, these terms relate to "the mystery of God." As long as I live, I shall never forget the plaintive cry of a young girl a few weeks before her bat mitzvah. I had been called to the family's home as her father had just passed away. She sobbed in my arms and cried out, "God damn You, God!"

Things happen in our lives that are incomprehensible! There is much that we cannot know that we wish we did. I don't believe we can understand the reason for everything. I resonate to God's ultimate response to Job when he finally demanded an answer from the Almighty for his many afflictions: "Where were you when I laid the foundations of the world?" (Job 38:4).

As human beings created in God's image, we have a very good idea of what God hopes our behavior will be. God hopes we will treat one another with graciousness and love. We may hope that God will likewise treat us with graciousness and love. There is still an infinite gulf between the reality of God and our knowledge of God. That is an essential element of my faith.

We do perceive, though, that God's love, grace, and salvation are things we must try to earn. This is one of the largest real differences between classical Jewish and classical Christian thought. In Christian thinking, faith in God and Jesus is indispensable if one wishes to gain grace, salvation, and God's unconditional love.

By contrast, we Jews believe that we must try to earn them through the acts of kindness, caring, and compassion that we do. Our belief in God, or lack of belief, is a secondary consideration.

We also believe, though, that because of God's graciousness and love for us, we have a mission to use Torah—understood in the broad sense of the term as all of Jewish learning—to work toward the salvation of the world. It is a goal we may never fully attain, but as Rabbi Tarfon taught, "We are not free to desist from it" (*Pirkei Avot* 2:21).

4

In recent decades we Jews—Reform Jews in particular—have submerged mention of the afterlife to the degree that many Jews frame the question to me as an assumption: "We don't believe in life after death, do we, Rabbi?"

I would respond, "Yes, we do!"

For Jews, attaining the reward in *olam haba* (עוֹלָם הַבָּא), "the world-to-come," does not depend on what we believe. It depends on how we live our lives.

My belief in life after death has two parts: what I hope and what I know.

I hope, and in my heart I believe, that good people receive in some way rewards from God in a realm beyond the grave. I hope that they are reunited with loved ones and live on with them in a realm free of the pain and debilitation that might have marked the latter stages of their earthly life.

My father died at age fifty-seven, and my mother, who never remarried, died at age eighty-eight. She was a widow for more years than she was married. My fondest hope since her death is that they are together again.

I cannot, of course, prove that any of this is true. Yet I cling tenaciously to my hope.

But there is also an aspect of afterlife of which I am absolutely sure. Our loved ones live on in our memories, and those memories can surely inspire us to lead better lives.

At the beginning of Noah Gordon's marvelous novel *The Rabbi*, the protagonist, Rabbi Michael Kind, thinks of his beloved grandfather, who died when he was a teenager, and recalls a Jewish legend that teaches, "When the living think of the dead, in paradise the dead know that they are loved and they rejoice" (Gordon, *The Rabbi*, 1).

Each time we do something worthy because of their teaching or example, our deceased loved ones come alive. If we listen, we can hear them call to us as God called to Abraham in establishing the sacred covenant of our faith: Be a blessing (Genesis 12:2)!

Study and follow God's instruction (Genesis 17:1)! Practice and teach those you love to practice righteousness and justice (Genesis 18:19)!

And then, when we turn their teachings into our actions, we know—we absolutely know—that our loved ones are immortal, and they live on in a very real and special way.

RABBI OREN J. HAYON

1

Any sustainable interpretation of the notion of *tzelem Elohim* (צֶלֶם אֱלֹהִים) cannot violate the core elements of God's identity. God's form is unknowable (Exodus 33:20), and God is not replicable (Exodus 20:4); indeed, in the Jewish tradition, God's identity is rooted in utter uniqueness. How, then, can we make sense of the suggestion that humanity shares God's likeness? If God's true self cannot be fathomed, let alone duplicated, how can it be said that human beings resemble God? The answer must be that the "image" we share with God cannot be understood to be a reflection of how God looks. Instead, our shared identity must inhere in something that exists above and beyond the form and function of our physical selves.

I find myself moved by Maimonides's assertion (in his *Guide for the Perplexed*) that humans' primary value can be found in our intellect. This is not to say that a smarter person is more valuable than an ignorant one or that impediments to learning must be impediments to holiness. Instead, it means that the divine image is rooted primarily in humans' capacity for imaginative creativity.

In their commentary on I Samuel 2:2, the Rabbis urge the reader to revocalize the Hebrew *tzur* (צוּר), "rock," a popular biblical metaphor for God that implies strength, power, and immovability, as *tzayyar* (צַיָּר), "creator, artist," encouraging us instead to prioritize

God's capacity to conceive, build, and animate (Babylonian Talmud, *B'rachot* 10a). The implication of their teaching is clear: more important than God's enormity and power is God's ability to create things where previously there was only chaos or void. We humans too are blessed with this ability, and it is our imaginative capacity that connects us to God. We may look, act, and reproduce like animals, the Rabbis teach, but humans are the only animals with the combination of high creative ability and the free will to bring new things into being.

Since, as noted above, the most significant component of God's identity is uniqueness, we are led to the paradoxical conclusion that this is the trait that we share with God: the holiest part of our humanness is that we, like God, are each utterly and undeniably unique and that only we share the godly potential to bring more novel and unique creations into the world. Perhaps the deepest appreciation of the concept of *tzelem Elohim* can be found in the dazzling range of human diversity. We resemble God precisely because the richness of our individuality, combined with our breathtaking creative capacity, is what makes us capable of bringing goodness into the world.

2

Those new to Jewish study are often taken aback by the sheer volume of legal text concerned with gender, sexuality, and reproduction. Of all the parts of human experience and human bodies, they wonder, why should sacred text be so extensively concerned with the functions of the most intimate parts of our bodies and the way they contribute to our identity?

It is true that Jewish tradition focuses a great deal of attention on the human capacity for fertility and reproduction. But this is not because our priests, prophets, and sages were puritans; they did not pay obsessive attention to these parts of human life out of an impulse to suppress sexual desire or behavior. Instead, our spiritual forebears were concerned with these issues because they recognized that our gender identity is firmly connected with the way we infuse growth, renewal, and hope into our human experience.

It is easy to infer a certain prudish anxiety from Judaism's historical conversations about gender and conclude that our tradition believes that the human body ought to be approached with disgust or fear. But in the end that reading fails. True, Jewish law focuses frequently and critically on the human capacity for reproduction and the roles and perquisites of human gender. True, Jewish tradition does not cringe from the reality that we are made of bodies, blood, and breath. For these reasons, some classical Jewish text may strike us as indelicate or even offensive. But we must remember that these texts direct us toward profound conclusions about the nature of the relationship between God and humanity.

The Jewish religious experience cannot be separated from the body. Torah asserts itself on even the most intimate and miraculous parts of us. According to the traditional understanding, the womb and the foreskin are primary loci of Jewish identity and Jewish covenant. While our liberal expressions of Judaism reject the notion that our gender must dictate our destiny, still we recognize that our genderedness provides a way for us to make God more brightly manifest in the world.

Gender is an essential and primary component of human life as characterized in Genesis 1:27, *zachar un'keivah bara otam* (זָכָר וּנְקֵבָה בָּרָא אֹתָם), "male and female [God] created them." These verses that describe the work of God the Creator are evidence of a daring and irrepressible religious message that was the Jewish gift to human history: our gender is the first gift we received from God, and so God must be intimately concerned with the products that emerge from our maleness and femaleness—procreation, pleasure, and the complex folds of social identity.

As our understanding of human gender expression grows more and more complex, we are reminded that this component of our identity holds the potential to reassure us of God's loving presence in the sacred processes of creation and renewal. Reproduction and intimacy are precious to God; as we explore these dimensions of human life, we become better acquainted with the Jewish truth that our bodies are not obstacles to spiritual life, but doorways into a deeper relationship with God.

3

The suggestion that Christianity, more so than Judaism, has a primary claim on grace, salvation, or love has a remarkable tenacity; the fact that it is false seems to have no effect on its longevity. Perhaps it is simply the case that a faith that accommodates the possibility of divinity made flesh makes it easier to imagine that God "loves" like a cherished spouse or "saves" the imperiled like a military hero. One need not perform intricate theological contortions to find a meaningful place for these terms in our modern Jewish lives; indeed, they have been a central part of Jewish thought all along.

After all, at their root, all of these terms are simply expressions of the holy possibility for one to value and prioritize someone else above oneself, and that kind of loving selflessness is a central trait of what Jews understand to be God's personality. *B'ni b'chori Yisrael*, God calls us—"Israel is My precious firstborn" (Exodus 4:22)—and we are instructed to recognize and imitate God's capacity for selflessness in our relationships with each other. Unlike the Christian theological perspective, Judaism does not assert that "salvation" is necessary to redeem us from sin or damnation, but instead, simply that the human capacity for love and generosity is the necessary precondition for us to create a just and sustainable world.

In the second blessing of the *Amidah*, the central liturgical unit of Jewish prayer, God is praised for the divine capacity to provide for the needs of humanity. The text declares that God personally undertakes the moral acts that are incumbent upon us as well: healing the sick, releasing the captive, and caring for the homeless and impoverished. God undertakes these kindnesses on earth and so merits the title of *matzmiach y'shuah*, the "One who causes salvation to blossom." When we come to recognize God's presence in acts of selfless goodness, we are reminded each time we pray these words that we—just like God—personally bring grace, love, and salvation into the world by living lives of virtue and generosity.

4

In his definition of *kareit* (כָּרֵת), the biblical punishment of "being cut off from one's people" (see, e.g., Leviticus 18:29), Maimonides diverges from the apparent plain sense of the Torah's text, which on its face seems to indicate that *kareit* is a kind of exile or excommunication from the Jewish people. Not so, Maimonides asserts; instead, we are to learn that God punishes the wicked by "cutting them off" from eternal life and instead dooms them to simply die "like the animals," while the righteous merit an eternal, blissful life after death (*Mishneh Torah, Hilchot T'shuvah* 8:1).

I am attracted to Maimonides's notion of *olam haba*, the afterlife, as a nonphysical, purely intellectual existence. This conception appeals to me morally because it serves as a reminder that a successful life is one that combines virtuous behavior with the eternally rewarding practice of intellectual exploration. I also find it psychologically comforting to contemplate that there is something about us that can endure beyond the grave. Whether the eternal component of humanity is our knowledge, as Maimonides asserts, or our legacy on earth, I find the notion of complete annihilation after death to be a chilling one.

This is not to minimize the rational challenges posed by the concept of an eternal inner soul that is a component of human identity or consciousness. The questions it raises (Where does the soul rest? Can it be damaged or removed? Do all humans have the same kind of soul? What about other primates?) are impossible to answer and threaten to undo the entire Jewish concept of the human soul.

Despite the intellectual challenges, however, I believe that there is a compassionate argument to be made in favor of the idea of an eternal soul. Too many human lives have been unfairly cut short by violence, disease, and injustice; too many righteous people from among us—and from all the peoples of the world—found no dignity as they lived and died and now lie in anonymous burial places. I find this truth devastating as well and want to believe—even though this belief is irrational and perhaps unsustainable—that a God of goodness will ensure that something of all of us will live on.

RABBI YOEL KAHN

1

Rabbi Akiva taught, "Great is God's gift of making us in the divine image. But even greater is the gift of knowing that we are made in the divine image" (*Pirkei Avot* 3:14). The essence of our humanity, according to Jewish teaching, is our awareness of being the representation—simultaneously both reflection and messenger—of the Holy One on earth. This knowledge produces a dialectic tension in ourselves and in relationship to others: on the one hand, this teaching affirms the fundamental dignity of each person, *qua* person; regardless of achievements or capabilities, every human is equally worthy and deserving of respect (see *Mishnah Sanhedrin* 4:5). Despite our ongoing, renewing mutual estrangement—whether between one person and another or between entire peoples—the "other" can never be completely demonized so long as I remember that they too, just like you and I, are imprinted with the image of God.

Yet our teachers, both ancient and modern, frequently counter this "essentialist" reading of our creation in the divine image because they find it excessively static. Martin Buber sees in the mythic story of Creation the summons to each person to grow and become: "Realization—this is the awesomeness of the covenant between God and [humanity]. . . . The first covenant with the lump of clay which the Creator, kneading, and by the breath of [God's] mouth, imbues with [God's] own likeness, so that it might unfold in [humanity's] life and thus reveal that not being but becoming is [the human]'s task" (Buber, *On Judaism*, 112). Buber does not specify how this "becoming" unfolds, but its outcome is the "realization" of the Divine on earth. Commenting on Isaiah 43:12, Rabbi Shimon bar Yochai explains that God declares, "If you are My witnesses then I am God. . . . But if you are not My witnesses, I am not, as it were, God" (*P'skita D'Rav Kahana* 12:6). This realization, known as *tikkun* (תִּיקּוּן), is simultaneously an individual task—as in the famous story of Reb Zusya, who is afraid of being asked upon his death why he was not "more like Zusya"—and a collective responsibility. The Jewish project—and, by extension, in our modern vocabulary, the human project—is collectively making real the fullest expression of the divine image already imprinted within and unfolding through our humanity. The fulfillment of this endeavor is neither more nor less than Judaism's messianic idea.

2

Jewish spiritual practice is forever celebrating, on the one hand, separation, division, and distinction and, on the other, integration and unity. The language of Jewish blessing focuses on rites of dedication and separation; the Hebrew *k'dushah* (קְדוּשָׁה) means "set apart, dedicated to a particular purpose." Thus, the Jews are a *goy kadosh* (גּוֹי קָדוֹשׁ), "dedicated nation," Exodus 19:6; and in the traditional marriage ceremony, the sexual and reproductive capacity of the wife is "set apart" and assigned to her husband: *at m'kudeshet li* (אַתְּ מְקוּדֶּשֶׁת לִי), "you are dedicated unto me." Similarly, food is dedicated for a particular sacred purpose, and only when it has been so designated may it be eaten.

Despite this celebration and lifting-up of acts of distinction, Judaism imagines that ultimately all separations will be erased. In Kabbalah, everything is rooted in the *Ein Sof*, the boundary-less Infinite One in whom there are no distinctions. Time, so central to Jewish consciousness, is dissolved, as we declare in the *Birkat HaMazon* (Blessing after Eating) on Shabbat, "Merciful One, help us to see the coming of a time when all is Shabbat." Light and dark are no longer, as the prophet proclaims, "A day is near that is neither day nor night" (Zechariah 14:7). Human differences are resolved, too, for "My House shall be called a house of prayer for all peoples" (Isaiah 56:7). On that day—when all human and natural distinctions are erased, when the cosmos returns to the state it was in before Creation began—only on that day shall "God be one and God's name one" (Zechariah 14:9).

It is against this background of ambivalence—on the one hand, elevation and celebration of difference and, on the other, the ultimate dissolution of all distinction—that we can speak of the conflicted place of gender in Judaism. Gender roles and gender awareness are at the core of the Creation story (and its subsequent interpreters) in Genesis 2; yet in the earlier Creation story in Genesis 1, gender is noticed but not core to the narrative. Both biblical accounts imagine heterosexual union as the momentary restoration of the mythic original unification. Jews today no longer imagine completion exclusively through marital union and are open to the dissolution of presumed gender differences and roles while honoring the distinctiveness of each individual.

The increasing visibility of transgender people among us is further challenge to the binary assumptions of our tradition and an invitation to a much broader challenge to these categories or their very existence.

3

Ahavah (אַהֲבָה), love, is the motivation for *matan Torah* (מַתַּן תּוֹרָה), the revelation of the Torah at Mount Sinai. Our daily liturgy reminds us of the "everlasting love," *ahavat olam*, which is expressed through the gift of "teaching us Torah and mitzvot, laws and precepts." Christian scripture reduces this rich, nuanced, and renewing suite of gifts to a narrow legalism, which it then replaces with its own substitute revelation. What Jesus is to Christians, Torah is to Jews. For Jews, as for Christians, God's most precious revelation is an ongoing, intimate Presence with which we continually engage. The Torah—in all its multi-vocality and complexity—is our Creator's loving gift and is the means by which we are enabled to navigate this life and this world.

Mutual love engenders mutual commitment. The Jew responds to the gift of revelation with the freewill offering of one's own love (Deuteronomy 6:5–9). Love, the passionate, full commitment of our spiritual and moral capacity to the service of the sacred, is what we are summoned to do. Yet if Torah is the expression or articulation of God's love for us, then our engagement with Torah—our wrestling, our interpretation, our renewal—is the route through which we express our love back to God. Accordingly, our study of Torah must be passionate and engaged, an ongoing and openhearted act of love—without compromise of intellect, science, or reason—through which we are led to deepen our commitment to the realization of its teachings; thus, "the study of Torah is equal to them all because it leads to them all" (*Mishnah Pei-ah* 1:1).

We aspire to the realization of all the Torah's teachings, to living with such integrity and purity of spirit and action that "the earth is filled with the knowledge of the Eternal as the waters cover the sea" (Habakkuk 2:14). This unreachable-but-ever-striven-for goal is the messianic era; yet, we learn, the Messiah will arrive the day before he/she arrives. Salvation comes from God, because we must confront our own human limitations and failings; but, paradoxically, God's presence and agency are expressed through our human action. Many of us have experienced "a taste of salvation" in different dimensions of our own lives (see Babylonian Talmud, *B'rachot* 57b) such that our faith in the possibility of ultimate salvation is grounded in our own lived experiences, no less than the Jewish tradition's grounding this faith in the experience of the Exodus.

4

We declare each day in the Morning Blessings, "*Elohai, n'shamah* (אֱלֹהַי נְשָׁמָה)—My God, the soul You have given me is pure." After the arrival of humanity at the end of the sixth day of Creation, "God then surveyed all that [God] had made, and look—it was very good!" (Genesis 1:31).

For the early Rabbis, faith in the immortality of the soul and the future bodily resurrection of the dead were essentials of Jewish belief—despite the complete absence of any biblical basis for either of these ideas. (This of course did not stop the Rabbis from creatively reading many different passages and stories in support of their teaching.) As a modern, scientific-reality-based Jew, I read the historical sources metaphorically and symbolically, no doubt as many, but surely not all, Jews have done for centuries.

The old *Union Prayer Book* eloquently expressed the historical Jewish teaching that our first and best legacy is the life we have lived and those we have touched: "The departed whom we now remember . . . still live on earth in the acts of goodness they performed and in the hearts of those who cherish their memory" (*Union Prayer Book*, 152). While I yearn to believe fully in the other Jewish ideas that follow, I can honestly say that this is the only "afterlife" of which I am confident and, as I grow older, am increasingly able to embrace as sufficient.

The Jewish narrative of exile and homecoming, so central to Jewish experience and Jewish imagery, also has shaped our people's imagination of what lies beyond. It was hard enough for the Jew to live in exile throughout this lifetime; Jews could not imagine being in exile for eternity. Accordingly, much Jewish teaching emphasizes that whatever follows, we are not alone, and the soul "comes home" to intimacy and safety.

A core teaching of modern science is that there is no loss of energy in the universe. When a drop of water returns to the sea, the level rises a little bit—even if we cannot measure it, nothing has been lost. The water, though, has returned to it source. Similarly, just as the water, carbon, and other elements within the body are returned to the earth, so does the human soul return to its source—for there is no loss of energy in the universe.

RABBI SUE LEVI ELWELL

1

Like life itself, being created in God's image is both a gift and a responsibility. This essential Jewish concept is a *prozdor* (פְּרוֹזְדוֹר), "an entryway," to Jewish life and Jewish practice. God created humans not to duplicate or replace the One who is unique, but to extend God's reach through righteous, just, and compassionate action. When we sing, *Ein k'Eloheinu* (אֵין כֵּאלֹהֵינוּ)—"There is none like our God," we are celebrating God's singularity. Like human twins, or parents and their biological offspring, individuals may share many similarities. But each individual is, finally, unique. So it is with us, created in God's image, yet other, reaching always toward our uniquely human potential to "be like God." As creatures of flesh and blood, we are created from dust (Genesis 2:7), and we will return to dust.

Judaism invites us, every day, to reach beyond our humble beginnings and to enter into conversation with God. Prayer offers us tools for expressing what the writer Anne Lamott calls "Help, Thanks, Wow" (Lamott, *Help, Thanks, Wow*), providing language for petition, gratitude, and praise. Jewish prayer reveals God's attributes and invites us to partner with God in imagining, building, and nurturing a more just and equitable world. When we sing *Nasim shalom* (נָשִׂים שָׁלוֹם)—"Let us make peace," we take our place as God's partners, created in God's image, striving to realize in this world God's goodness, God's generosity, and God's loving-kindness (*tovah, chein, chesed v'rachamim*—טוֹבָה, חֵן, חֶסֶד, וְרַחֲמִים).

A first step toward realizing these goals is by seeing ourselves in God's image. For some of us, this is the work of a lifetime. Because we are dynamic and ever-evolving individuals, we return, again and again, to this goal: seeing ourselves as God's partners. And just as we work toward seeing ourselves as reflections of holiness, our perspective on the world changes when we begin to consider every individual, every human being, as created in God's image. Our tradition gives us language to express our amazement when we encounter the Divine Presence in every soul: "You are Blessed, Holy One, who has such creatures in the world! You are Blessed, Holy One, who varies Creation!" When we see ourselves, and every other, as a mirror of the Blessed Holy One, we may glimpse what the world looks like through God's eyes. This is our gift, our sacred opportunity.

2

We are living at a time of amazing discoveries about the beauty and the mystery of human creation. Most of us were educated to see human beings as a binary universe, divided up neatly into male and female. The first question asked when a new soul enters the world is often, "Is it a boy or a girl?" Myriad assumptions follow when the infant's sex is announced. But sexual assignment, that is, immediately apparent physiological characteristics, does not always correlate with gender, the social roles and behaviors that are most natural, comfortable, and life-affirming for each individual.

Jewish tradition has long understood that the categories of male and female are insufficient descriptors of all people. The Mishnah introduces the categories of *androgynos* (אַנְדְּרוֹגִינוֹס), someone with both male and female sexual characteristics; *tumtum* (טוּמְטוּם), an individual with neither fully developed male or female genitals; *aylonit* (אַיְלוֹנִית), an individual who was assigned female gender at birth but later developed male characteristics; and *saris* (סָרִיס), an individual who was assigned male gender at birth but lacks male genitals, either since birth or due to a medical intervention.

Our ancestors understood that gender is more complex than male and female and that each of us may carry characteristics that are dominant and recessive. Until the middle of the last century, however serious Jewish study and teaching, as well as community leadership and representation, were the sole province of men and those who were accorded male privilege. Thankfully, that has begun to change in most corners of the Jewish world. It is nevertheless important to listen to the voices of the past to mark our progress—or lack thereof—in ensuring equal access to Jewish life, Jewish text, Jewish community.

In 1912, Bertha Pappenheim, a German Jewish social justice pioneer and historian, wrote,

> The house of study—the home and nursery of specifically Jewish culture—has ever been closed to the woman . . . thus, not only in the past, have we been referred always to the male concept of the Torah, the commentaries, and the tradition. . . . We Jewish women must take, unquestioningly, praise and blame, admiration and condemnation of the sex, as we get it scattered through the vast masses of literature, through the spectacles of male scholars, who read into Jewish literature their own personal opinion and personal experiences. (Pappenheim, "The Jewish Woman in Religious Life," 160)

One hundred years later, we must ensure that our Jewish study includes the voices, the interpretations, and the wisdom of women and men, of transgender individuals, and of those who identify as gay, lesbian, and bisexual. We are all created in God's image. Each of us must be a full partner in the conversation about what it means to be fully human and fully Jewish.

3

We named our first born Hana (חַנָּה) in gratitude to God's graciousness in bringing this infant into the world and to express our amazement at the grace that emanated from and surrounded this perfect being. In the Torah, and in contemporary Hebrew usage, the phrase *limtzo chein* (לִמְצוֹא חֵן), "to find grace or favor," is used when referring to individuals finding favor in God's eyes, people being received by one another with grace or favor, and God ensuring that the Israelites will be welcomed and treated fairly by other peoples. Our behavior and our interchanges with others shimmer with energy and purpose when we become conscious of reaching toward or mirroring God's *chein* (חֵן). And when we regard one another as if looking through God's eyes, everyone we encounter becomes surrounded by the light of *chein*.

Y'shuah (יְשׁוּעָה) is more than physical rescue. Particularly in the language of Psalms, *y'shuah* is divine deliverance. While contemporary Jews may not say, "I've been saved, delivered, rescued," we may feel that an intervention we might attribute to a higher power has helped us from slipping away into despair or depression. We may see the kindness of another as God's hand reaching out to us when we had abandoned hope. *Y'shuah* invites deep conversation about the timing of events, encounters, and opportunities in our lives.

The *Sh'ma* (שְׁמַע) is often the first prayer that Jewish parents teach to their children. After declaring that God is One, we continue with *V'ahavta* (וְאָהַבְתָּ), "And you shall love." This prayer, which occurs twice in the daily liturgy, commands us to love God. We may be surprised and challenged by this directive. How can we be commanded to love? By introducing our children to Judaism with these words, repeated as a bedtime ritual, *V'ahavta* becomes an expression of the love and care that young children associate with the safety and security of parental protection and home. Interestingly, our tradition teaches that while we are commanded *to love* God, we are commanded *to respect* our parents. Because our parents are, like us, fragile human beings, they, or we, may not be able to feel or express love. *V'ahavta* welcomes each of us to discover a love that transcends human frailty, passion, and desire, a love that is more powerful than even the love of a mortal parent, a love that is more powerful than death.

4

I was born into a loving family, and I remember my dad saying the *Sh'ma* with me every night when I was a child. My ritual continued, "God bless Mommy, God bless Daddy . . . ," adding everyone in my family and extending the list as long as I could to make sure that Dad would stay in my bedroom as long as possible. I remember the night I realized that my father's father was *dead*. It hit me hard. How could my father be in the world when his father, my grandfather, was *dead*? I still remember my sense of disbelief, incomprehension, and fear.

I am now a grandmother myself. And my dear father, who cared for each of us with such intention and devotion, is no longer living. Yet my father lives in me and in each of us who were privileged to know him. When we remembered him at a simple memorial service and as we gathered each night for a week of *shivah* services, we shared stories and memories and anecdotes of a life well lived. And now, a year later, each of my father's children and especially my mom, my father's devoted partner of sixty-five years, carries him in our hearts every day, as we go about our lives, interacting with others, using words that we learned from him, making decisions that are influenced by his choices, his values, his deep commitments, his Judaism.

My father's soul lives on through the worldviews of each of us who were privileged to learn from him. We, his heirs, bear the most precious legacy: his words, his deeds, his admonitions, his hopes.

I believe that God's mind is an endless vault filled with memory banks that will never be erased. We mortals are challenged: *zachor* (זָכֹר)—*remember* those who have come before us. I am trained as a historian; we must sometimes spend months and years archiving the past to discover parts of the truth that happened before our own day. But no truths are ever completely lost; no souls are ever truly gone. God holds all our stories, all our secrets, all our loves, all our joys. Those who love us may access some of the stories, some of the truths. But in the end, each moment has meaning, even when we ourselves cannot parse that meaning. God collects those moments, and savors them, and saves them. The Holy One, whose presence transcends time, will keep our souls for all eternity.

RABBI JAY HENRY MOSES

1

Human beings partake of the divine image in three principal ways: through the power of creation and destruction, the faculty of speech, and the ability to love.

One of the great mysteries of human life is how we get here in the first place. Our ability to create new life inspires awe precisely because we sense that something more profound than simply a biological process is at work. The Torah portrays the creation of humanity as the pinnacle of God's work. The fact that we "partner" in this supreme act is perhaps our most intimate connection to God. We, too, are creators, bringing forth new life and then devoting ourselves to shaping that new life into a covenantal being.

Similarly, we possess both the drive and the ability to be destroyers of life. Though our tradition commands us to curb and limit our destructive impulses, the power we have to control the fate of our planet and the creatures that inhabit it derives from our source in the Divine.

The faculty of speech is commonly understood to be what separates humanity from the "lower" species. One of God's names in Jewish tradition is "the One who spoke and the world came to be." As described in Genesis 1, God creates the world through speech: "God said, 'Let there be light!'—and there was light" (1:3). In God's image, our faculty of speech can be a force for both creative and destructive forces. When we speak words of wisdom, care, and love, we create hope, goodness, and life. When we speak words of cruelty and insensitivity, we can destroy reputations and lives.

Finally, our capacity to love is the most unique and profound aspect of humanity being created in God's image. God's love is understood to be expressed through the gift of Torah (see *Ahavah Rabbah*, in the morning liturgy). The highest expression of our humanity is when we feel love for another human being and that love motivates us to share selflessly and to put someone else's needs above our own.

God did not *need* to create humanity; but the Torah shows a God with love to give and in need of a partner upon whom to bestow it. We are that partner—imbued with the awesome power to share in creating new life, to create worlds with speech, and to touch the realm of the infinite when we love.

2

The *Zohar*, the great canonical work of medieval Kabbalah, is suffused with profoundly gendered imagery. It is a work that is self-consciously claiming to be an expression of the deepest, most hidden wisdom about the nature of the Divine. On that deepest level, God has both masculine and feminine traits, aspects, and energies. Sometimes these male and female energies are in uneasy tension or conflict with each other. Other times, they are in harmony. This poetic image has cosmic consequences. For the kabbalists, in other words, gender is a key that unlocks the deepest mysteries of the universe.

The image the kabbalists are drawing upon is, first and foremost, the Creation story in Genesis 1, where God creates humanity "male and female," simultaneously, in one act of creation. Some traditional sources have understood this to be an androgynous single being; others have pictured a being with two faces, male and female, facing opposite directions. This last image was taken up by the mystics to be a metaphor for the alienation and distance we so often feel from each other and from God. Men and women struggle to connect, human beings are often "facing away" from our fellow human beings, we feel distant from God while God pines for us, and the world remains in an unredeemed state.

Conversely, the great hope lies in a day when our male and female "faces" will turn and be able to see each other. Of course, this requires a painful separation of what was once a unified being with two faces; it must be separated into two beings, at first increasing the alienation. But once separated, these beings have the ability to turn and face each other. The climax of the *Zohar*, its resplendent image of a world where humans know God's deepest will and are in sync with the order of Creation, is represented by male and female energies coming together in love and harmony, employing the divine power of Creation.

When we can harness the mysterious power of gender, using it not as a tool of power or subjugation, overcoming the innate distance and alienation its overlay can impose upon us, we can achieve our most sublime states of human existence: redemption and peace.

3

We need to rescue the concepts of "grace," "salvation," and "love." Rescue them from what? In the twenty-first century, we should be ready to revisit the Jewish people's relationship to Christianity. Deeply rooted in our psyches are the fear and anger born of centuries of outsider status among Christian majorities and religious persecution, sometimes officially sanctioned by the church. One unfortunate result of this deep unease has been a tendency among Jews to distance ourselves from many core Jewish ideas and images, merely because Christianity adopted them at some point and they came to take on a Christian overtone. Our fear took over and a word like "grace" became *t'reif* (unkosher). It's time to remedy that. We live in a time of unprecedented religious freedom for most Jews and a great openness to honest interchange with Christianity. We have nothing to fear, and we should reclaim our lost religious language.

But there is another rescue operation required for these particular terms. They were shunned in much Jewish discourse not only because of their associations with Christianity but also because they all imply a personal relationship with God. Our decisive encounter with nineteenth-century rationalism added to our unease with these terms: modern, rational, Western, enlightened people did not countenance a God who showed them personal grace, saved their souls, or embraced them in love. We are the grandchildren of these self-consciously rational Jews. We have seen rationalism's strengths, and we know its limitations. As religious people, we need a God to whom we can relate in human terms, even as we know that those terms apply to God only metaphorically. For too long, we shunned anthropopathism, the imbuing of God with human emotions. The result was that many Jews came to feel so distant from God that we struggled to have any sense of God's presence in our lives at all. We are sophisticated enough to pray for God's grace, salvation, and love—because these ideas reflect our deep human needs—without mistaking these poetic images for literal, simplistic requests of a God who is "like us, only more so."

4

Death is the greatest mystery. Judaism insists, above all, that just as life is not meaningless or random, so too death is a meaningful part of our existence, not an end but a transition in an eternal story.

The mystics of our tradition teach that each of us has within us a divine spark. This spark is what connects us to our ultimate Source, God, the great light that gives off the sparks. A related image is that God is the root system of our souls. Each of us is connected to the infinite in this way, where God is the source and we are the manifestation. In this view, death is merely a returning to the great source (light, root) from which we came in the first place.

I believe that to be a religious person, at its most basic, is to assert that we are part of something greater than ourselves. If we are bound by the limits of our senses, our intellect, and our time in this earthly realm, then the something greater of which we are part must transcend all of these limitations. There must be more to the story than this life.

But I also believe it to be meaningful that we are *not* granted access to what that eternity or afterlife may consist of, how it works, or in what way it is connected to our earthly, time-bound consciousness. Death is the great mystery precisely because our inability to know what lies beyond forces us to focus on how we are living here and now.

So, yes, the conventional wisdom is true: Judaism, with all its mitzvot, customs, and ethics, is focused primarily on how we live our life in the present, and less so on *olam haba*, "the world-to-come." Still, our great texts are studded with reminders that there is an incomprehensible depth to our existence and that God's vision of the world goes infinitely far beyond the scope of any one life.

In the face of the great mystery, the religious Jew asserts not that he knows exactly what awaits him; merely that there is a Source out there and that the prospect of returning to that Source offers enough comfort to confront the abyss of the unknown.

RABBI DEBRA J. ROBBINS

1

Being "made in the image God" can be a motivating idea, an inspiration to emulate God's actions that lead to blessing. This capacity encourages us to visit the sick, as God visited Abraham after his circumcision; to feed the hungry, as God provided for Hagar and Ishmael; to forgive, as God forgave the Israelites for the terrible transgression of the Golden Calf. We till soil and tend vegetables as God planted in the Garden of Eden. We send donations to causes we care about, to help bring about freedom, as God freed the Israelites from the narrow confines of Egypt. We even write, bringing individual letters together to fill pages recording our history, imagining a better future, inscribing our memories and ideas like God's Torah.

Being made in the image of God encourages us to imagine ourselves as embodiments of at least the seventy images of God (Baal HaTurim, *B'haalot'cha* on Numbers 11:16). Too often in our arrogance we reflect the image of *Melech HaOlam* (מֶלֶךְ הָעוֹלָם), "King of the World," or in our desire for power we emulate *Adonai Tz'vaot* (יְיָ צְבָאוֹת), "Lord of Hosts or Warrior," or we push beyond the natural and steady image of God as *Tzur Yisrael* (צוּר יִשְׂרָאֵל), "Rock of Israel," into intractable stubbornness. *Tzavaat HaRivash* invites us to consider the image of God as *Dak min HaDak* (דַק מִן הַדַּק), "the Most Delicate and Exquisite of All," constantly at our side (*Tzavaat HaRivash* 137,

The Testament of Rabbi Yisrael Baal Shem). This image, the Most Delicate and Exquisite of All, is like an intricate spider's web sparkling in the sun after a rainstorm, like a scrap of gold-glimmering crocheted lace, like a piece of finely crafted shimmering silver filigree jewelry. We can become entangled with this God, feel this Presence on our skin, wrap this God around us like a shawl or tallit, wear this God as a sign around our hands or on our fingers, clasped gently around our necks. *Dak min HaDak* is eternally and infinitely permeable, accessible and tangible—human beings, always and everywhere, wrapped up in the image of God, each one wearing a unique and eternal invisibility cloak charged with holiness.

2

Standing at the base of Mount Sinai, everyone is free. It is a singular inspirational moment in time when all are equal, when the possibilities for men and women are endless. In that moment, we glimpse our potential to shape a sacred society where everyone is together, each person valued, regardless of gender, sexual preference, physical, spiritual, or emotional differences; each person, made in the infinite images of God, respected for the holy gifts he or she contributes. The unity of Sinai is fleeting. There are struggles over power and authority. Who will have the courage and the integrity, the relationships and the language, to overcome the anxiety, to bring the people together and lead them forward, with God, toward a new way of loving and living? Often the narrative focuses on the role of men, but when we read closely, we see the actions and hear the voices of women, enriching and diversifying, deepening the connections of the community.

Wandering in the wilderness, Miriam leans in from the shadows of the story. Early in Exodus, she had a prominent role, rescuing her brother Moses and bringing joy to the celebration of freedom. And then she is not only silent but invisible. Finally, partway into the Book of Numbers, we see her body and hear her voice. Miriam joins with Aaron and together they speak out publicly and critically of Moses. Harsh consequences follow that afflict only Miriam. Some commentators suggest this is a warning to women—don't try to be too powerful, or raise your voices too loudly and publicly, or think you have the power to lead (Eskenazi and Weiss, *The Torah: A Women's Commentary*, 862–83). But the story ends in a way that changes the world. Moses leans in and prays for Miriam. The entire community leans in, setting out only when Miriam returns to their midst as a leader.

We are the descendants of this community, of Moses *and* Miriam. It is time to stop wandering and struggling. There is room for all the voices, for all the ideas, for the leadership of men and women. Every day is an opportunity to stand again, unified, with respect and awe at Sinai. Each one of us can lead. All of us can respond. We can all lean in and together change the world.

3

My grandparents, of blessed memory, were married for more than sixty-five years and early on agreed to disagree about God. My grandfather embraced classical Reform Judaism, abandoning personal ritual practices like tallit and kashrut, taking up in their place the ethical principles of social justice—causes of civil rights, equality, literacy, and Zionism. Showing boundless love for all people (*ahavah*, אַהֲבָה), seeing with grace the inherent goodness in all others (*chein*, חֵן), and working to bring about salvation (*y'shuah*, יְשׁוּעָה), understood as freedom, were daily and personal expressions of his faith, as God's partner here on earth. God may have acted in these ways long ago, but now the work is up to us, my grandfather taught us. His faith was expressed not in personal prayers or petitions to God but in real life—appointments on calendars that showed time spent with people he loved, checkbook entries to causes that brought freedom and redemption to those who were not yet free, looking at each and every person he encountered with deep respect and generosity.

My grandmother taught us something different. Her focus was on her very personal relationship with God. She talked with God, in the synagogue and at home, praising and petitioning God to see with *chein* (inherent goodness or grace) those who needed it, to shower *ahavah* (boundless love) on her loved ones, to bring *y'shuah* (salvation), to intervene in life, like in biblical times, with redemptive miracles to free us from narrow places of personal struggle. In the twentieth century, these rich and ancient Jewish concepts with nuanced Hebrew meanings were translated into accessible English and embraced as actions we humans could take to repair God's broken world. Now, in the twenty-first century, we continue to be God's partners in repairing the world, and some seek, in addition, a more personal and intimate partnership with a gracious, loving, saving God.

My grandparent's marriage is instructive because it was able to hold both of these approaches. Their relationship allowed for a diversity of interpretation, theology, and action—and perhaps as a result was strong and enduring. Our communities and families, our lives and our world, can be stronger and better if we can affirm, as they did, each in their own unique and respectful way, that *chein*, *ahavah*, and *y'shuah* are expressions of human action in God's world *and* expressions of God's actions in our world.

4

In yoga class we do an exercise where we imagine holding a basketball in our hands. With minds focused on the present, feet planted, and hearts lifted, with our hands we trace the shape, push against the edges, even toss it into the air and catch it. We can feel the ball even though we can't see it; we interact with it even though it is not there. The same is true of the souls of our loved ones after they have died.

At the first *Yizkor* service led by Rabbi Sheldon Zimmerman, nearly twenty-five years after my mother died, he taught something that has taken me twenty-five years to understand: "Our relationships with our loved ones continue even after they are gone." Like the basketball at yoga class, we can't see them or feel them, but we can hold them, and our relationships with their souls, with our own souls touched by them, continue.

For many years I thought my soul, the sparkling sacred essence of who I am, was a response to my mother's death, that I am who I am because she died, that I took on her soul when we buried her young body. But now I know that isn't entirely true. I have my own soul, formed and shaped, expressing my own values, dreams, and personality, breathed into me by God on the day I was born, not on the day she died. I am a wife and mother, a friend and a rabbi, not only because my mother died when I was a child, but because in the eleven years that we had together in this world, she shared her soul, her passions and commitments, with me—*and* because in the years since I have made them my own. She was clear and consistent about her core values, and they endure and find new expression in my life: hospitality, Jewish life in America and Israel, teaching and learning, nurturing friendship, being part of a complicated family, expressing creativity, being organized and in charge. With my feet planted, as I breathe deeply, focus quietly, lift my heart, feel confident and supported, I can see her soul and my own. I feel and embrace our ever-evolving and deepening relationship, life and after-life, breathing together for eternity.

RABBI JUDITH SCHINDLER

1

Being created in the image of God gives us human rights. The Talmud teaches that all human beings were created from one human being so that no person can say, "My ancestor is greater than yours" (*Sanhedrin* 37a). The Sages add that we were created "from the four corners of the earth—yellow clay and white sand, black loam and red soil—so that the earth can declare to no part of humanity that it does not belong here, that this soil is not its rightful home" (*Yalkut Shimoni* 1:1). We were created as equals. Each one of us is deserving of our God-given humanity, dignity, and equality.

Being created in the image of God gives us responsibilities. We are required to honor the image of God in all human beings and create a world that supports, rather than subjugates, the stranger in our midst: the one who is unknown to us or the one whose difference seems strange. Race, religion, weight, ability, sexual orientation or identification, and country of origin are just a handful of the differences that create the colorful quilt of our congregations, country, and world.

Being created in the image of God gives us creativity. Genesis requires us to be co-creators and partners with God in completing Creation.

Being created in the image of God means we must strive to actualize that which is godlike in ourselves. In our sacred texts, God embodies the ideals for which we strive. God pursues peace. God demands justice. God acts with mercy.

Rashi teaches that being created in the image of God means that we are endowed with the qualities of understanding and discernment. May we develop these traits. Nachmanides notes that being created in the image of God reflects our immortality. May we work not only for the present but for the future so that our labors on behalf of others and the lessons we teach our children live on. The midrash teaches that God originally created human beings with two faces and then divided them (*B'reishit Rabbah* 8:1). Just as we can see God in the seventy faces of each and every verse of Torah (*B'midbar Rabbah* 13:15–16), so too can we see a God in the face of every human being. Being created in the image of God means we are inextricably bound to all creation, for God dwells in everyone and everything.

2

In God's image, male and female, God created the first human being. The concept of gender is woven into our image of God and into the fabric of Creation. As a sacred text, Torah binds us together as Jews and inspires us to live by the highest ideals. As a humanly authored text, Torah portrays God according to its contemporaneous understanding of gender. As one example, Torah identifies God as *rachum* (רַחוּם), "compassionate." The root letters form the word *rechem* (רֶחֶם), which means "womb," thereby connecting God to the image of a mother, nurturer, and creator of life. Elsewhere, God is described as *Adonai Tz'vaot* (יְיָ צְבָאוֹת), meaning "God of hosts or armies," reflecting a male militaristic God who protects His people and roots out evil. God commands not only the heavenly hosts but also the earthly armies who fight on God's behalf.

The kabbalists teach that the Hebrew name *Adam* for the first human being comes from the Hebrew *adameh* (אֲדַמֶּה), meaning "I will be like," from Isaiah 14:14, which reads, "I will be like the Most High." Adam strives to make himself like God, and all of us who are descended from him strive for the same. We have human bodies with godly souls. To be fully human is to actualize the potential with which we were created. We are not meant to limit our aspirations of embodying only the female attributes of God if we are woman or the male attributes of God if we are man. Today, we see sexes crossing traditional lines of work and ways of being. Women can be soldiers and scholars, and men can be healers and homemakers. Being human means mirroring the full spectrum of God's attributes (*midot*, מִידוֹת).

I am a fraternal twin, and in a small way, my birth was likened to that of the first human being. Male and female, my brother and I were brought into this world. While we joke that we are polar opposites, our differences are never related to gender. It was our social, academic, and professional paths that varied.

According to Rashi, the *tzeila* (צֵלָע) that was taken from man to create the first woman should be translated as "side" rather than the more commonly used "rib." Man and woman were two sides of one being and then divided. The wholeness (*shalom*, שָׁלוֹם) for which Jews strive cannot be achieved by acting alone. Bringing perfection to our world is not about realizing one's own specific gender traits but rather about collaborating with others to maximize God's worldly reflections. Our goal is to nurture within ourselves those traits, whether traditionally male or female, that will help us better our world and be effective partners in completing Creation.

3

Living in a southern city with hundreds of churches, I hear the terms "grace," "love," and "salvation" regularly spoken at social events. In Christianity, these attributes are God's gifts, which from the human perception may be undeservedly given. One needs to deeply desire them, and God will respond as a parent who unconditionally loves, forgives, and saves a child. Even the most hardened criminal need only repent in his heart and these divine rewards will be attained. In Judaism, God's attributes of justice and mercy both come into play. As Moses and the Israelites learned after committing spiritual adultery by building the Golden Calf, God's forgiveness, grace, and love must be earned through our actions of repentance and repair (*tikkun*, תִּיקּוּן). Being rewarded for the good we have done, rather than being punished for the pain we have caused, is based on our actions.

Living in the South has taught me about "southern grace," which entails hospitality, etiquette, and appearing your best: writing thank-you notes and offering up sweet tea. In all religions, but especially Judaism, God demands more. When the prophets of our faith approached God in petition (as in Abraham's plea to save the innocent of Sodom), they prefaced their request with the phrase *im matzati chein b'einecha* (אִם מָצָאתִי חֵן בְּעֵינֶיךָ), "if I have found favor [literally, 'grace'] in Your eyes." God's grace is earned through actions of justice and goodness.

In Judaism, salvation is not about saving souls but about saving our world. The title of Rabbi Robert Levine's book, *There Is No Messiah and You're It*, captures our human responsibility for bringing about deliverance. I believe that merely praying for a savior and waiting for salvation will get us nowhere. We can open doors as a gesture of hospitality; we can open doors as a ritual act as we do for Elijah at Passover; or, we can truly open doors to the oppressed so that their rights are attained, and to the hungry and homeless so that the structures that perpetuate economic inequity are rebuilt on the foundation of justice.

Love, in Judaism, likewise finds its primary expression in human beings rather than emanating from God. Love, like prayer, requires reaching out in three directions. We must reach inward and love ourselves. We much reach outward and love others. We much reach upward, not in the literal direction but in spiritual aspiration, and love

God by loving God's Creation and by bringing the ideals of our religion into reality.

4

In Genesis, God created *Adam* (אָדָם), the first human being, from *adamah* (אֲדָמָה), the earth. God then breathed the breath of life into that first individual. Our bodies, our physical and genetic composition, were formed by our biological parents. Our souls were given to us by God and nurtured by those who raised and taught us. Just as the ark is the sacred vessel that houses our Torah, so is the body the sacred home to our soul. Both the Torah and our souls transcend time.

Albert Einstein is often cited for quoting the law of conservation of matter and energy: "Energy cannot be created or destroyed, it can only be changed from one form to another." I believe that the energy that forms our soul does not die. As a rabbi, I accompany congregants on their end-of-life journey. With them, I walk to the edge. I witness their bodies weaken as their souls remain strong until their last breath. Reflecting Einstein's theory, I believe the energy of a person's soul doesn't die. It lives on in the universe. Perhaps it returns to God. Perhaps, as the mystics of the Kabbalah teach, it makes another *gilgul* (גִּלְגּוּל)—another circle through life as it lives, learns, and strives for godliness.

While one's soul living on after one dies is a matter of faith, living on through the legacy we leave is matter of fact. I rely on both when it comes to keeping alive the spirit of my own father, Rabbi Alexander Schindler, of blessed memory. Rabbi Yochanan said in the name of Rabbi Shimon bar Yochai, "Every scholar who is quoted in this world, his lips whisper from the grave" (Babylonian Talmud, *Y'vamot* 96b–97a). Among the many ways that my father's words live on are through his teachings that people continue to quote. Through the transformative Interfaith and Outreach Initiative that he envisioned in 1987 as president of the then-UAHC (now URJ), he is brought to life every day in synagogues across the globe. On a mystical level, too, my father's soul speaks to me. My father was my teacher and mentor, who taught me how to craft sermons and eulogies and how to be a rabbi. When exhaustion overcomes me and I don't know how to find the words to soften the pain of those experiencing a tragedy or inspire a congregation on a holy day, a divine energy and my dad's energy move me forward. In the same way that we can connect with God as a wellspring of healing and strength, so can we connect with the soul energy of our loved ones after their breath/soul (*n'shamah*, נְשָׁמָה) leaves them and returns to its Source.

RABBI STANTON ZAMEK

1

Much is being said when we assert that human beings are created in the divine image. To say that we are made *b'tzelem Elohim* (בְּצֶלֶם אֱלֹהִים) is to make a radical statement of human equality, a vital message in a world riven by invidious distinctions that weight the value of some over others. The concept of creation in the divine image cuts through and ultimately invalidates all human classifications, providing a "God's-eye view" that reminds us that each soul is infinitely precious.

Equal in this context does not imply identical, however. Creation *b'tzelem Elohim* is also a radical statement of individuality. The Sages tell us that it is an aspect of the greatness of the Holy One that God uses the same "stamp" to mint human beings and yet, unlike a human coin maker, produces something unique each time (*Mishnah Sanhedrin* 4:5). There is a spark of the Divine within each human being, but the iteration of God within each human soul is an unrepeatable revelation. To denigrate or marginalize another is thus an act of blasphemy, a rejection of an aspect of the Divine that can be found nowhere else.

Seeing the human as the image of the Divine brings with it a duty of respect and even reverence of others, but it also entails a duty to the self. The Mishnah tells us that we must be able to say, "For my sake was the world created" (ibid.). I take this as a charge to see our own soul as a manifestation of God in the world, a sacred presence that we are bound to explore and express as best as we are able. We reach out to God by reaching inward, by seeking the wisdom inscribed within us from the very beginning of our existence.

We say in the *Birchot HaShachar* (morning prayers), *Elohai, n'shamah shenatata bi, t'horah hi* (אֱלֹהַי, נְשָׁמָה שֶׁנָּתַתָּ בִּי, טְהוֹרָה הִיא), My God, the soul You have given me is pure. This is not to say that *we* are pure. We humans have an enormous capacity for folly. We harm ourselves, we harm others, and we stray far from God. And yet, because we are made *b'tzelem Elohim*, there is that within us that cannot be sullied. The soul is of God. It can be occluded, its light can be hidden, but the soul in essence is always *t'horah*—it is pure. As such it is a beacon continually pointing toward life and blessing, and away from death and curse. We have been given all we need to live a holy life. The soul within us is a candle in the window guiding us home.

2

The mystery of gender is encoded in the first two verses of Genesis 5, in which we read, "This is the book of the lineage of Adam: On the day God created the human (אָדָם), in the image of God He created *him*. Male and female He created *them*, and He blessed *them* and called *their* name humankind (אָדָם) on the day *they* were created" (Genesis 5:1–2, trans. Alter, *The Five Books of Moses*, emphasis added). The Rabbis noticed the fluidity of person and gender in this passage and posit that this indicates that the first human creature was an *androgynos*, a dual entity that was both male and female. This being was later separated into man and woman (*B'reishit Rabbah* 8:1).

This midrash is a mythic representation of a profound truth. Male and female both are and are not one. All of humanity is created in the divine image. The essence of us, men and women, is genderless, pure soul. There is a fundamental unity of humanity that transcends gender. Yet we are clearly not the same. We inhabit the world as gendered beings, as one aspect of the primal being and not the other. Thus while there is much that men and women share in terms of their understanding of this life, some experiences are bound to gender. These can be communicated across the gender divide, but there are men's truths and women's truths accessible to each alone.

We are then dependent on our fellow humans of the opposite gender for a full view of our existence. The need for egalitarian and inclusive communities follows from this. The price of deafness to the voice of the "other" is intellectual and spiritual impoverishment.

Gender is perhaps the most fundamental manifestation of the diversity we experience within the unity of humanity, but it is not the only one. Ben Azai taught that "this is the book of the lineage of Adam," the prooftext for the common origin of the entire human family, is "a great principle of the Torah" (*B'reishit Rabbah* 24:7). Indeed it is, and yet there are still differences that matter. We of the family of Adam see the world through the lenses of a multitude of ethnicities and faith traditions. No one person has access to the totality of the human experience. As the myth of the androgynous Adam helps us navigate the divide between male and female, so it speaks to the diversity of culture and faith. At the most fundamental level, humanity is one body. The peoples of the world differ, but in the way male and female differ—not of necessity or by design in conflict, but with the potential to be complementary and to be something greater together.

3

Often when we question the relevance of a theological category or idea in contemporary Jewish life, obsolescence is not actually the issue. The problem is dissonance. The tradition remains relevant, but its message is often profoundly countercultural. It appropriately challenges the assumptions of our age.

So in a time dominated by a sense of entitlement, the concept of *chein* (חֵן), "grace," is extraordinarily valuable. It speaks a truth that needs to be heard—that every day we are the recipients of blessings that we do nothing to earn. At our more honest moments we know this to be true. We know that we endure through God's mercy, that we depend not on ourselves but on the fact that it is God's nature to give. That is why we end *Avinu Malkeinu* with the plea "Be gracious to us and answer us, for we have no merit." Our psyche should not be dominated by such self-effacement, but the religious personality must have room for an appreciation of one's smallness in relation to God. This perspective is provided by an understanding of God's grace.

Laboring as we often do under a false sense of self-sufficiency, salvation too is a necessary counterpoint to the secular ethos. As progressive Jews, we cannot accept a stance of pure quietism where we simply wait patiently for God to redeem us, but we are justly skeptical of the idea that humanity alone can perfect this world. If we have hope that the ills of this world can be healed, there is no alternative but to posit that our efforts are in partnership with God. If hope is relevant in contemporary Jewish life, then so is salvation.

As for love, the time has surely come to cease ceding this ground to our Christian brothers and sisters. Judaism is a religion of love. It seems strange to have to assert this when we affirm this truth every time we recite the *Sh'ma* and Its Blessings. From the beginning of our Jewish education we learn to recite "You shall love the Eternal your God with all your heart, with all your soul, and with all your might" (Deuteronomy 6:5). This declaration of our love of God is immediately preceded by an assertion of God's love for us, a love given concrete expression through the gift of the Torah.

This is covenantal love, a love buttressed by mutual obligation. It is a love that asks more from us and from God than feeling alone. It is a love that is to be demonstrated through action. And yet there is an emotional component here as well. The bond of love between God and Israel transcends the promises we have made to one another. God's loves endures, even when the covenant is strained. We continue to love despite unmerited suffering, both personal and communal. We remain "more eager for the Eternal than watchmen for the morning" (Psalm 130:6).

4

The soul is the connection point between the human, in the most individual sense, and the Divine. My soul is me in essence, my truest self and the image of the Divine within me. While my psyche is susceptible of being distorted and corrupted, the soul, being of God as well as of me, remains pure. I can do much to hide this light within me. I can so encrust the soul with sin that no one can see it, including me. Yet it endures in purity.

Our godly soul gives us the power to effectuate our own redemption. No matter what we have done, no matter how dark the path we have walked, we can peel away the *k'lipot* (קְלִיפּוֹת), the spiritual occlusions of the soul, and be truer to the image of God within us.

As I believe that the soul is of substance with the Divine, I affirm that it cannot die. I believe that there is an existence that follows earthly life. What this existence is, I cannot say. I take all teachings concerning *olam haba* (עוֹלָם הַבָּא), "the world-to-come," to be metaphors for a reality beyond human conception. I understand none of them to be a literal map of the terrain of the next world. I do not know what the afterlife is in essence. Most of the time it is sufficient for me just to know that it is.

In his brilliant book *The Death of Death*, Neil Gillman writes, "I tend to minimize the popular notion that one's immortality rests in the memories one leaves behind, in the impact of one's life on friends, family, and community, in children and in grandchildren, in the institutions one helped build, the students one taught or the books one published" (Gillman, *The Death of Death*, 244–45). I share this dissatisfaction with such notions of "practical" immortality. While the language and images I use to communicate my belief in a life after this one may be metaphoric, they point to something real, just as the expressions I use to discuss the Divine, however inadequate, point toward the Living God.

In part it is my belief in God as a real, conscious presence separate from the material world that leads me to belief in the world-to-come. Having made this first enormous leap, it is relatively easy to come to the conviction that death does not separate me from my God. To posit that death severs my connection to God is to posit a God too small for my theological needs. I find myself in agreement with Gillman that "if God is truly God, if God's will and power are absolute, then God must triumph over death as well" (ibid., 259).

I of course cannot know these things in a rational sense. These are convictions I reach through *chochmat halev* (חָכְמַת הַלֵּב), "the wisdom of the heart." Song of Songs says that "love is as strong as death" (8:6). This deeper way of knowing tells me that love is stronger.

RABBI BEN ZEIDMAN

1

"God now said, "Let us make humanity in our image, after our likeness . . ." (Genesis 1:26). To offer one of our tradition's many explanations for the use of the words "us" and "our," Rabbi Yaakov Culi teaches that to assist with the process of Creation, God created three artisans: heaven, earth, and water. These three were given tasks and the power to complete them. Water retracted to make space for earth. Earth created the heavenly lights. Heaven caused the firmament to come into being, separating the water below from the water above. Everything that was created came to fruition via the efforts of these three artisans. Finally, on the sixth day, they came to God ready to receive the next set of instructions. "But God said to them, 'On this day I wish to create the most significant creature in all the universe, Humanity. None of you alone has the power to accomplish this, as you did the other things in creation. You must all work together, and I will join you. You will provide the elements for humankind's body, while I will place in him a holy soul" (Culi, *The Torah Anthology: Me'am Lo'ez*, 1:108–9).

With that in mind we look to the very next verse, which begins, "So God created the human beings in [the divine] image . . ." (Genesis 1:27). Everything other than humanity exists thanks to the basic elements of our world. We, however, represent something unique and different from *anything* else. The question we have asked since the beginning of time is, Why? Why are we here? Why are we the only creatures like us? The answer Jewish tradition offers is that we are made in the divine image.

This is not merely an explanation. It is a calling. That piece of holiness within each and every human being explains why we have obligations to take care of our world. Why we look after plants and animals that show no concern for us. Why we time and again break from animalistic self-preservation and self-concern to look after those in need of help. To be created in the divine image means all of us are capable of behaving in divine and holy ways, and we therefore have the responsibility to do so.

2

Not to be confused with the term "sex," "gender" refers to the "socially constructed roles, behaviors, activities and attributes that a given society considers appropriate for men and women" (World Health Organization). Whether we define gender as binary (either male or female) or as a spectrum, the key concept that we all must understand is that humanity is gendered, whereas the Holy One exists beyond such a socially created earthly constriction.

Jewish tradition, along with the rest of the world, has throughout history had very specific ideas of what it means to be a man or a woman. Responsibilities and expectations have been divvied up strictly (and often stiflingly). As what it means for us to behave like a man or a woman thankfully shifts and our tradition is reexamined for a modern era (as must continually be done), it remains true that human beings live life in a world defined in large part by gender.

Again we look at this verse from Torah, "So God created humanity in [the divine] image, creating it in the image of God, creating them male and female" (Genesis 1:27).

> Rabbi Jeremiah ben Elazar taught: At the time when the Holy One created Adam, he was created androgynous, as it is written, "Male and female God created them." Rabbi Shmuel bar Nachman teaches that at that time when Adam was created, he had two faces. Then the two sides were separated so that two complete beings were created. (*B'reishit Rabbah* 8:1)

In this version of the sacred origin story, both sexes were created at once, and therefore gender definition would have been unnecessary. All human beings are created in the image of God no matter their gender identity. Gender is an aspect of *this* world, not of the heavenly realm; it is part of what makes us fully human rather than godlike.

Gender plays a key role in our lives, in how we interact with the world. We are beautiful in our ability to emulate the Divine through the human lens, and one of the many ways in which we approach our world is through the kaleidoscope of our personal identity. Gender is one of the many things that make each of us unique and special individuals. We are not meant to *be* God, only to be capable of behaving in godlike ways. We do not have to accept society's definition of appropriate gender roles, but at the same time gender is one of the many parts of who we are that enables us to do wondrous and amazing things.

3

In the Hebrew Bible, *chein* (חֵן), "grace," is a term applied to both human beings and God. Theologically, "God's grace" refers to God's willingness to show us mercy and to grant us blessings. It's a challenging proposition for many modern Jews who don't accept the idea of divine reward and punishment. Yet, by rejecting this idea outright, we miss the opportunity for the corollary notion that human beings can be gracious as well. In treating one another with kindness, in showing favor and compassion to others whether it is deserved or not, we emulate the Holy One. We can be God's hands in making our world a better one. That too is a form of grace.

"Salvation," *y'shuah* (יְשׁוּעָה), represents the general idea of being saved. The very first line in the Song at the Sea, just after the Israelites make it across the sea, begins, "God is my strength and might; God is become my salvation" (Exodus 15:2). The word, however, later comes to mean not only communal salvation, but also personal salvation. As with the term "grace," this connotation is challenging for those who have let go of traditional notions of divine punishment and reward. Salvation in Judaism comes through the process of personal repentance and atonement (never through an intermediary). Jewish tradition teaches that we can lean on God as support and even as *savior*, because when we truly seek salvation with all our being, we find it. As we read on Yom Kippur, "Great is penitence, for it brings healing to the world, as it is said, 'I will heal their affliction, generously will I take them back in love' (Hosea 14:5)" (Babylonian Talmud, *Yoma* 86a). Our Rabbis teach that God is always waiting for us to turn back to righteous living. The way back is always available to us.

Love, *ahavah* (אַהֲבָה), takes two. Strangely enough, we are *commanded* to love in one of our most special prayers, the *Sh'ma*: "You shall love *Adonai* your God with all your heart, with all your soul, and with all your might" (Deuteronomy 6:5). At the same time, Rabbi Akiva explains when asked to teach the Torah on one foot, "Love your neighbor as yourself, this is the greatest principle in the Torah" (Jerusalem Talmud, *N'darim* 30b). Love is something that we do for one another, that we do for God, and that God does for us. In loving one another, we make our world a better place. In loving God, we strive to dedicate our lives to creating communities in which the Holy One would want to dwell. In striving to feel God's love for us, the burdens and the challenges we face in life may feel a little less overwhelming. A life of love is a meaningful and fulfilling life.

4

The soul is that which makes us unique in this world. Touched by God, it cannot be described by mere words. It may be better understood by looking at what the soul *provides.*

The soul gives us the ability to consciously experience how amazing our world can be. Moments of wonder and amazement (as Abraham Joshua Heschel teaches) and of encounter (as Martin Buber teaches) are recognized by human beings because we are unique among the creatures of our world. The soul is the slate that we strive to cleanse on Yom Kippur; it is the reason we feel good as we do acts of loving-kindness even though we ourselves do not benefit.

The afterlife is a conundrum I admit I will never understand. To know the afterlife is to be there! And yet, Jewish tradition throughout the ages has expressed a number of different ideas on what happens after we die. Liberal Jewish thought focuses more on this life than on the afterlife; the focus of our lives should be how we live it in this world. However, those moments when the soul's presence is recognized encourage us to consider possibilities of what may come next. When we have holy encounters in our lives, occasions of profound encounter with something we realize is grander than we previously understood the world to be, we inevitably become concerned with how we (and our souls) fit into the larger framework of our universe.

The morning prayer *Elohai N'shamah* makes mention of the afterlife. The traditional liturgy for this prayer reads, "You have preserved [the soul] within me, and You will take it from me in the future, then return it to me for the world-to-come. . . . Blessed are You, God, who returns souls to dead bodies." Troubled by the nonrational notion of physical resurrection, the early Reformers preferred the idea of spiritual immortality (Petuchowski, *Guide to the Prayerbook*, 53–54). So the first Reform Jewish prayer book includes the following instead: "Thou hast preserved [the soul] in this body and, at the appointed time, Thou wilt take it from this earth that it may enter upon life everlasting" (*Union Prayer Book* [1924], 65).

I understand these words to mean two things. First, we have the power to touch people's lives beyond our own comprehension. I never met my great-grandfather Samuel, but he had an affect on my grandmother, who affected my mother, who affected me. In my life and in the lives of every single individual he ever came across (and each of their descendants), he lives on just as every single soul that has ever come into this world lives on eternally.

Second, perhaps our spiritual soul returns to its Source and unites with the Holy One. But I prefer the tradition of Antigonus of Socho: "Do not be like servants who serve their master for the sake of receiving a reward. Rather, be like servants who serve their master without the intent of receiving a reward. And let the awe of heaven be upon you" (*Pirkei Avot* 1:3).

Section Three

ON THE JEWISH PEOPLE

1. As liberal Jews who value religious autonomy, how are the concepts of "covenant" (בְּרִית), *b'rit*, and "commandment" (מִצְוָה), *mitzvah*, relevant to us? In what way is the Torah sacred text for us?

2. What is a Jewish definition of "being religious" or "having faith"? How does communal prayer fit into the definition?

3. Does the Jewish people have a unique vocation among the nations? Do you affirm hope in a "messianic age" (יְמוֹת הַמָּשִׁיחַ), *y'mot hamashiach*?

4. Are Jews obligated to enter into dialogue with members of other faith communities? If so, on what basis and toward what end?

RABBI GEOFFREY W. DENNIS

1

In response to Christian claims of human "sinfulness," many Jews cite Genesis 1:31, "God then surveyed all that [God] had made, and look—it was very good!" as proof that Judaism regards human nature as essentially good. Yet in Genesis, humanity is newly born. It is being alive that is very good, but being alive in itself is not the essential human experience. The key to being human appears at the end of the Torah, not at the beginning, at the point where, having matured under God's parental eye, we are preparing to go forward into a promising but unknown land—let's call it "adulthood." In Deuteronomy 30, we are informed that every human being must choose their direction in life. From this we learn that we are neither innately good nor evil, but innately free. It sounds paradoxical, but the Torah takes our freedom as a given, a Jewish value that is best expressed in our own times by Reform Judaism.

That being said, no one has total autonomy. We are born embedded in circumstances beyond our control: genes and gender, geography and family, resources and law, what we know and what we don't. We grow in a chrysalis of inherited relationships—personal, political, and cultural. Beginning with a life where much is given and little is chosen, we grow only gradually from our infantile goodness into our mature freedom. And like people everywhere, Jews must exercise our autonomy within the framework of all these relationships and inheritances.

As Jews we have a unique inheritance—Torah: an ancient relationship, a *b'rit* (בְּרִית), a contract with God, not of our choosing, that nonetheless affirms our utter freedom. In fact, it demands we choose. It asks us to voluntarily commit ourselves to a project, to a set of moral and social ideals (mitzvot) utterly grounded in human freedom, even as that project urges us toward something even higher—holiness—a state where the divide between what is human and what is divine starts to dissolve.

This quest for *elohut* (אֱלוֹהוּת), "divinity," through holiness, while personally rewarding, is not a purely personal journey, because that would too easily devolve into narcissism. The Torah declares, *k'doshim tih'yu, ki kadosh Ani Adonai Eloheichem* (קְדֹשִׁים תִּהְיוּ כִּי קָדוֹשׁ אֲנִי יְיָ אֱלֹהֵיכֶם), "You all [plural] shall be holy, for I, *Adonai* your God, am holy" (Leviticus 19:2), emphasizing that we can achieve this project only in a communitarian context. For this reason, Judaism calls us to choose community over isolation. It insists that *chevrah*, *k'hilah*, *avodah* (חֶבְרָה, קְהִלָּה, עֲבוֹדָה), "society, synagogue, and communal worship," are the vehicles by which a Jew makes that journey from goodness to freedom to holiness.

2

Habakkuk declares, *v'tzaddik be-emunato yich'yeh* (וְצַדִּיק בֶּאֱמוּנָתוֹ יִחְיֶה) (2:4). That can be translated as "The righteous shall live by *faith*," but also as "And the pious are rewarded with life for *fidelity*," or even "And the just by *confidence* live." The equivocal meaning of this verse captures the equivocal, problematic Jewish relationship to the Western idea of "faith" and the closely related English word "religion." Both fail to truly encompass the Jewish experience, in which ethnicity and religion, faith and fate, being and becoming, eternity and history, belief and deed, all overlap, intertwine, and stand apart from each other like a hopelessly tangled rope or like a multidimensional Venn diagram.

Over the years I've come to realize that to be a Jew is less analogous to being a Christian or a Muslim, a person with a set of beliefs, and more akin to being a Navajo or a Hindu. We are less like a group of co-religionists and more like a global aboriginal people with its own unique, endless, and endlessly varied spiritual tradition that informs the way in which we move through the world. One God, one Ground of Being, yes; but with many ways in one tradition to become a *tzaddik* (צַדִּיק), one who is righteous, pious, and justified. So how do we "live" this tradition in a way that is righteous, that honors our God and our own spirit? Through the varied possibilities expressed in the *emunah* that Habakkuk speaks of. Not "faith" but "fidelity," fidelity to our people and its history; not "faith" but "trust," by trusting in our God; not "faith" but "confidence," by having confidence in our people's purpose and in our Jewish selves.

3

One of the axioms of Torah is that God draws meaningful distinctions. We may choose life or death, but God prefers that we choose life (Deuteronomy 30). So too, it seems, God would prefer that Jews choose to remain Jewish. One would assume this divine preference is not mere caprice, but because there is a purpose to our physical continuation. Lately I have come to think about a connection between this divine need for Jews and another axiomatic Jewish idea: that the future will be better than the present—the *y'mot hamashiach* (יְמוֹת הַמָּשִׁיחַ), the "age of the Messiah." In its traditional form this envisions an inspired person, a physical descendant of King David, initiating a transformation on a global scale. This "redemption" will terminate the destructive cycles of war, inequity, and oppression and herald the dawn of a more perfect world.

Early Reform Judaism discarded this seemingly supernatural idea of an individual Messiah in favor of a progressive vision of collective humanity, to be spearheaded by the "ethical monotheism" of the Jewish people, which would bring about global redemption. A half-century and two world wars later, the Reform philosopher Steven Schwarzschild pointedly asked how the belief that all humanity could unify enough to achieve messianic aims was any less miraculous in its assumptions than was the belief that it could be accomplished by a single extraordinary person (Schwarzschild, *In Pursuit of the Ideal*).

There is a third way of thinking about these issues, one that reconciles both the necessity of Jews and the aspiration for *tikkun olam*, for both issues are actually grounded in a theology of embodiment, a theology that recognizes that our physical bodies have religious significance. An embodied theology simultaneously validates the importance that there be an "Israel of the flesh," because of the exponential power inherent in collective activism to improve our world, and the significance of the personal Messiah, which affirms the value of the individual and his/her potential.

So I ask: is not every Jew David's heir? I actually mean that genetically, not just figuratively. Consider the mathematics of the many children of David and Solomon reproducing over 150 generations, and surely almost every Jew living now is, in fact, a biological descendant of the Davidic line. I find the implications compelling. You embody the Messiah! I don't, as a convert to Judaism, but my children do; yours too. Not everyone is the Messiah, but most Jews are qualified to be. It's a strange thought, I admit, but such an embodied theology points us toward what I consider a very Reform conclusion: everything, from the survival of the Jewish people to the very redemption of the world, really does depend on you, on me, on all of us.

4

From its very beginnings, Israel has understood itself to be distinct and singled out from among the surrounding nations (Silberstein and Cohn, *The Other in Jewish Thought and History*). This has led some Jews to conclude that social isolation, to the maximum degree practical, is mandated by Torah. Yet the very arrangement of the biblical canon radically contextualizes any Jewish notions of uniqueness by beginning with the creation of all humanity and establishing the emergence of Israel through a proto-historical process (Genesis 1–Exodus 12). The entire Book of Genesis, in fact, provides the Jewish reader with ample sympathetic non-Jewish characters to relate to and identify with.

Moreover, the most exulted claim, that we are created *b'tzelem Elohim* (בְּצֶלֶם אֱלֹהִים), in the divine image (Genesis 1:27), is ascribed to all humanity, never merely to the Jewish people. Therefore all Jews are to think of themselves first as human, and related and equal to every other human (*Mishnah Sanhedrin* 4:5). Malachi's reminder to the Israelites that "everywhere incense and pure oblations are offered in My name; for My name is honored among the nations" (1:11) by itself makes dialogue with other faiths theologically appropriate.

Our shared humanity also has critical implications for the Jewish project of *tikkun olam*, bettering the world. While it is our doctrine, it is not ours alone to realize. The physicist David Deutsch describes humanity as the "universal explainer" and "universal constructor"—that in the known multiverse, only humans are capable of understanding and transforming all physical objects that are understandable and transformable (Deutsch, *The Beginning of Infinity*). Deutsch offers this as a materialist theory, but I think it represents the best modern characterization of what is meant by *b'tzelem Elohim*; we alone are able to be co-creators with God. And for all the wit, intelligence, and ingenuity to be found among Jews, there is an even larger body of "wisdom among the nations" (*Kohelet Rabbah* 2:13) of which we can and should partake. This obligates us to work with, and not just on behalf of, all people. It is the necessary way, *the only way*, for our goal of bringing *y'mot hamashiach* to realization.

RABBI DENA A. FEINGOLD

1

Because I cannot accept the idea that God literally imparted commandments to us in written or oral form at Sinai or any time since, the concept of mitzvah is difficult for me. Traditionally, the term mitzvah implies that God, a Divine Commander, promulgated laws by which we, the commanded ones, are to live. I do not believe that God makes the divine will known to us in this direct kind of way. Torah for me is a voice out of our ancient past, but it is the voice of human beings who were in some way inspired by God. With W. Gunther Plaut, I believe that "God is not the author of the text, the people are; but God's voice may be heard through theirs if we listen with open minds" (Plaut, *The Torah: A Modern Commentary*, xxxviii). It is this divine inspiration that explains the Torah's eternal relevance, meaning, and ongoing ability to teach and touch people. It speaks to us from the ages like a cherished letter, written in the hand of a loved one long ago, but still transmitting a message for us today.

The *b'rit* (בְּרִית), or covenant, concept, then, involves not an external relationship with God but rather an internal sense of obligation. We are in a covenant with others, with our people and with society, and indirectly, through those, with God. We are obligated to uphold our end of the covenant. We hope to get an equal response from others and, ultimately, from God, but it does not always work out that way. This can be disappointing, but disappointment does not exempt us from our obligation to the *b'rit.*

While I do believe that we are in a covenant with God, as described above, I do not see God as having a direct role in defining the terms of the covenant in the form of mitzvot. God is a Source of ethics and goodness that is within us and beyond us in the universe. Our heritage as a people, our history, and the generations of Jews who came before us are the forces that command us. Mitzvot are the sacred obligations to history, peoplehood, and heritage that we observe, as our hearts dictate, growing in such observance, by study and practice, throughout our lives.

2

Prayer reminds us of the values and ideals we should hold dear in our lives. When we come together to pray as a community, we affirm that we, as a people, are committed to shared values and ideals and that we will work together to uphold them. Prayer is both speaking and listening; but most of all, it is contemplating and imprinting our highest values, ethics, and dreams onto our souls. Music transports us and enlivens us in this effort. Fellow worshipers' voices support us. Creative readings and spaces for silence bring us opportunities for *kavanah* (כַּוָּנָה), "fresh intention," and new insights. Holy words, echoing through the Torah and haftarah readings and the ancient Hebrew prayers, link us with our people from ages past and Jews throughout the world today.

Having faith or being religious means committing ourselves to the ongoing Jewish endeavors expressed in communal prayer. Depending on individual practice, we affirm these endeavors each day, weekly, or on holidays, when we come together as a community to pray. Many of us find God in this process. We discover and are able to link ourselves to a Power in the universe or in ourselves that enables us to carry forward the values we profess in our prayers beyond the worship space. For others, faith may not be found in God or a Divine Power but in connecting to a heritage and a feeling of transcendent meaning, discovered with or without prayer.

It is unfortunate that many in Israel and America today use the word "religious" only to refer to Orthodox practice. Israeli semantics offer two options: that one is either *dati* (דָּתִי), "religious," or *lo dati* (לֹא דָּתִי), "nonreligious," with no middle ground—just two ends of a spectrum with nothing in between. Although I am not observant by Orthodox definition, I am religious in the following way: The synagogue is central to my life; Shabbat is observed weekly in my home through the values of *m'nuchah* (מְנוּחָה), "rest," *oneg* (עֹנֶג), "joy," and *k'dushah* (קְדוּשָׁה), "holiness"; I mark the holidays in significant and festive ways; Jewish study is a regular habit; and Jewish friendships are deeply important. I work to improve the world because I believe that such work is a Jewish imperative.

3

Affirming hope in a messianic age enables me to rouse myself to take time outside of my family and synagogue commitments to address justice issues in the broader community. I believe strongly in the theological concept put forth in the *Aleinu* section of each worship service: *l'takein olam b'malchut Shaddai* (לְתַקֵּן עוֹלָם בְּמַלְכוּת שַׁדַּי), that the world can be perfected through our human efforts. But, the concept of a personal Messiah—a single great human leader bringing us to a messianic age—is not part of my theology. Rather, I believe that human beings, working together to eradicate the problems we create in the world, can bring about a perfected world.

Having worked closely with people of all faiths for decades, I cannot say that we Jews have any greater calling or vocation than people of other faiths in this regard. My role models in this work come from all faiths: Abraham Joshua Heschel, Martin Luther King Jr., Sister Helen Prejean, and Mahatma Gandhi are a few who come to mind. As a participant in an interfaith, community-organizing group, I am often inspired by leaders of other faiths whose words or actions move me to higher activism in the work of justice or *tikkun olam*, repairing the world. I am also inspired in such work by political leaders or non-religious social activists. And although I do not see Judaism or religion as being uniquely situated to better the world, I do see it as a highly influential and important source of the initiative to bring justice and peace to society.

The Jewish people do, however, have a unique motivation among the nations. The teachings of Torah and the Sages and the concepts of *tikkun olam* and the *y'mot hamashiach* (יְמוֹת הַמָּשִׁיחַ), "the messianic age," inspire us to demonstrate that the world as we know it can be transformed by human action, in partnership with God. It is our unique vocation as Jews to share our texts and communal dreams with others, to act upon them in consonance with others, and to model the human role in creating a better world. Isaiah's concept that our people are to be "a light to the nations" (Isaiah 42:6) is an important text for me. The metaphor of light, with its connotations of enlightenment, illumination, and warmth, symbolizes for me the special role that we as Jews ought to play in working with others toward the perfection of our world.

4

Because we often have been misunderstood and maligned as a people due to ignorance, interfaith dialogue should be among the highest Jewish callings. The goal of dialogue is to educate, for both parties to be heard and understood. Over the years, with members of my congregation, I have been in dialogue groups with various groups of Protestants, Muslims, and Mormons. I have conducted many teaching seders at

Catholic churches and have given countless tours and talks to student groups and others about Judaism. I have been an active member of our local clergy association. I never tire of the opportunity to share what we believe and who we are as a people and to learn the same from others. Through these experiences, I have found that the nearly universal response to sharing Judaism is appreciation and admiration for our concepts and traditions.

In addition, in the high school level of our school, we have placed a high priority on exposing our students to other religions (and to other branches of Judaism as well). Living in a community where we are a small minority and most of our daily encounters are with people of other faiths, I feel it is essential that we inculcate in our youth a sense of familiarity with and respect for the faith traditions of those around us, as well as the skills to explain our beliefs and customs to others. Our history warns us of the perils of Jewish insularity.

When community issues arise, an interfaith group can most successfully address them when a relationship is already established. National or international conflicts can be discussed more easily when trust and comradeship already exist. The Muslim-Jewish dialogue in which I participated tackled the question of the Israeli-Palestinian conflict only after many months of sharing and bonding over religious practices, faith, and values—and amazing potluck meals. When this issue came to a head, it still was a difficult conversation, but a possible and productive one. This too can be an outcome of dialogue.

RABBI MICHAEL S. FRIEDMAN

1

Torah is sacred because it is the unique record of our struggle to understand the nature of God and the nature of human existence over the course of generations. For us, Maimonides says that the entire Torah has two simple purposes: *tikkun hanefesh* (תִּיקּוּן הַנֶּפֶשׁ), "repair of the soul," to develop positive character traits, and *tikkun haguf* (תִּיקּוּן הַגּוּף), "repair of the body," to understand truth about life (*Guide for the Perplexed* 3:27).

In other words, our tradition is a guidebook to living a better, fuller, more meaningful life. The paths that help us navigate our world are mitzvot. The traffic lights that regulate our progress are Jewish life cycles and milestones. The signs that direct us are Jewish values and Jewish wisdom.

Jewish ritual helps us become our best selves. Unfortunately, the term "ritual" gets a bad rap. It makes us think of something done by rote, without a true sense of intentionality or deeper meaning. But the purpose of Jewish ritual is precisely the opposite. A mitzvah—a Jewish act—is a way to put our most important values into action. For example, lighting Shabbat candles is not, in the end, just about lighting Shabbat candles. It is about marking the end of a hectic week with a quiet flame. It's about looking into the faces of our children and our companions because the rest of the week we're just whizzing by one another at warp speed. It's about reminding ourselves that we are to be beacons of light in an often dark world.

Jewish ritual can be a treasure. In order to experience its value we must know what it feels like viscerally, sensually, and emotionally. Jewish ritual can be a way to give in to our deepest longings: our longing for a moment of calm in a hectic life, our longing to disconnect—even just for a few minutes—from our devices and screens, our longing to shut out the noise and clutter and focus on what truly matters, our longing to reconnect with our spouse or with old friends, our longing to make a difference. Jewish ritual transforms us by making us more aware, more compassionate, more connected to one another. We don't observe mitzvot in order to be more Jewish; we observe the commandments in order to be more human.

2

When people are curious about what led me to choose to become a rabbi, people often inquire, "Was your family religious?" Perhaps they assume that anyone who decides to become a rabbi must have grown up in a home *very* different from theirs. They use the term "religious" to refer to all sorts of traditional rituals that they do not practice. In fact, my upbringing was probably not very different from theirs. We were members of a large suburban Reform congregation; my brother and I went to public school; we ate ham. But we also had Shabbat dinner every Friday when I was young. My brother and I both went to Jewish nursery school. Hebrew school and confirmation were non-negotiable. *Yahrzeit* candles were lit on the anniversaries of our great-grandparents' deaths. Shul was a comfortable place for us because we came to services at least once a month, if not more. Judaism was, in the words of Rabbi Andy Bachman, "an organizing principle of our lives." This was what set our family apart from others. And so I tell those who ask, "I grew up in an observant, religious, committed Reform Jewish home." For liberal Jews, living a religious life means living a life defined by Jewish values, Jewish wisdom, Jewish actions (mitzvot), and the Jewish calendar.

Faith, however, may be something completely different. At the end of the Coen brothers' film *A Serious Man*, a pimply, anxious thirteen-year-old is sent to the rabbi emeritus's office to receive a blessing on the morning of his bar mitzvah. The ancient rabbi wheezes and coughs from behind his desk and stares at the boy for what seems like an eternity. Finally he chokes out lyrics to Jefferson Airplane's "Somebody to Love," the same words with which the film began: "'When the truth turns out to be lies, and all the hope within you dies . . .' Then what?" The rabbi is pointing to one of the essential truths of Judaism: where all the certainties leave off, that is where faith begins.

For many liberal Jews, faith is treated as binary: either you believe or you don't. Moreover, we often look with jealousy upon those (often evangelical Christians) who speak about faith with admirable certainty. Since we are not exactly sure what we believe, we conclude that we do not believe much of anything at all. However, that is an unfair standard to hold ourselves to. Faith, as social anthropologist T. M. Luhrmann points out, originally meant something akin to "hold dear." It stood for our most important core values, rather than a scientific true-or-false. Communal prayer is one way to remind ourselves of those values: appreciation of the wonders of Creation, longing for comfort or peace, remembering those we love who are no longer by our side.

3

Why be Jewish? Why stay Jewish? Why live Jewishly? Our ancestors probably had little choice in the matter. Their identity was fixed, unchangeable. Ghetto walls and social intolerance confined them. But that is not the case for us.

Leon Wieseltier said, "To be a Jew is not to be an American or a Westerner or a New Yorker. It is its own category, its own autonomous way of moving through the world" (quoted in Pogrebin, *Stars of David*, 159).

The Jewish people still exists because in every generation there have been Jews who believed that our existence as a people and what we bring to the world *matters*. By all odds, we should have disappeared long ago, as many other peoples did. But we are here because we know that Judaism brings something essential to our lives—something that we cannot get anywhere else, something that animates and drives and comforts us. No matter the struggles or the successes, Judaism asserts that at the end of the day what we do with our time on earth matters. And it helps us determine how best to use that time.

Abraham Joshua Heschel put it best: "We are God's stake in human history" (quoted in *Time*, March 14, 1969). I don't think that statement is hyperbole. *Tikkun olam*, the Jewish duty to repair our broken world, arises from the observation that the world is fundamentally out of order; that everything is *not* okay. Despite their pervasiveness, corruption, inequality, and violence are each a divine injustice, a serious breach in the way God intended things.

Visitors to the Anne Frank Haus in Amsterdam are greeted with an excerpt from Anne's writings: "Who knows, maybe our religion will teach the world and all the people in it about goodness, and that's the reason, the only reason, we have to suffer. We can never just be Dutch, or just English, or whatever; we will always be Jews as well. And we'll have to keep on being Jews, but then, we'll want to be."

As Rabbi Jerry Davidson said, "[We are] a people that have endured [and], in spite of everything, have never failed to hope and to dream" (excerpted from *Temple Beth-El of Great Neck Bulletin*, September 1988). That is our unique role in the world. And that endurance, that hope, will inspire us to create the messianic world of our dreams.

4

For a number of years I coordinated and led an interfaith program for Jewish and Catholic teens called Project Understanding. The culminating experience each year was a study trip to Europe or Israel. Without fail, at a certain point—usually about four days into the trip—the students would exclaim, "We get it, Rabbi! You're trying to teach us that we're all the same!" I liked hearing them say that—not because it was accurate but because it enabled me to make an important educational and theological point. "No," I would respond. "It's exactly the opposite. I'm trying to teach you that Jews and Catholics are very different. But we share responsibility for the world." That shared responsibility for the world is both the basis and the end for interfaith dialogue.

Furthermore, we know that we Jews are but a small fraction of the human race. If we are to fulfill Isaiah's vision of being a "light to the nations" (42:6), we must be in dialogue with those other nations. We are obligated to enter into dialogue with good people of faith because only with partners can we possibly hope to bring light into a world that often seems so very dark.

RABBI GEORGE D. GITTLEMAN

1

My notion of *b'rit* (בְּרִית), or "covenant," functions on both the horizontal plane, between one Jew and another, and the vertical plane, between God and the Jewish people. The *b'rit* is most alive for me on the horizontal plane, in the sense of tribal responsibility Jews can feel for each other by being a part of *Am Yisrael* (עַם יִשְׂרָאֵל), "the Jewish people."

I feel this bond not just with Jews themselves but also with our heritage. Our obligation to follow the traditions of our ancestors is driven not solely by their divine origin but rather by our own need, as a people, to connect with and depend on those who came before us. The *shalshelet kabbalah* (שַׁלְשֶׁלֶת קַבָּלָה), "the chain of Jewish tradition," is not just about what God "said" or "commanded"; it is also about how our past experience has shaped who we are today.

On the vertical plane, between us and God, the concept of *b'rit* becomes considerably more challenging. In light of our tortured history, I struggle to accept the traditional understanding that the covenant detailed in the Torah governs the history of the Jewish people to this day. However, jettisoning the idea of covenant or chosenness is an equally unacceptable option. In doing so, we cast ourselves off into the chaos of history and lose any opportunity to ascribe meaning to our suffering and purpose to our existence. My approach is to "to build a heart with many chambers" (*Tosefta Sotah* 7:12). In one of them, I place the literalist view of covenant and election, and in another, I live my doubts, born out by history and affirmed by reason. In a third compartment, I nurture a more practical notion of covenant, as a way to make meaning and give hope as we journey through the vicissitudes of time and space. Depending on my need, I access one of those chambers.

Torah is the incomplete record of ancient Israelite life, lore, law, and mythic history, reflecting our ancestors' best attempt to write down and pass on their encounters with the Divine and what they believed were their most salient developments as a people. On the horizontal plane, the Torah binds us to our origins as a people and provides a foundation for who we have become as an evolving civilization.

The Torah is a living covenant when we bring our lives to it and challenge it to respond.

2

Rabbi David Hartman has taught that in this age of doubt and antagonism toward religion, just the desire to pray is a prayer in itself. This radical redefinition of prayer aptly describes what it means, from a liberal perspective, to be a religious Jew, "in the game," in dialogue with Judaism and Jewish life. One may question, argue, disagree, and doubt any and all elements of our tradition, but as long as one is leaning in rather than walking away from the myriad of challenges Jewish religious life poses, one is "religious."

It's instructive to note that Rabbi Hartman's definition of prayer ignores the question of "faith" and focuses rather on the religious act of prayer. Like our mythic ancestors who in response to their overwhelming sense of God's presence at Sinai said *Naaseh v'nishma* (נַעֲשֶׂה וְנִשְׁמָע), "we shall do and [then] we shall understand" (Exodus 24:7), faith is born out in our actions rather than in our theology. We work toward *tikkun olam* (תִּיקּוּן עוֹלָם), "repair of the world," because it is the right thing to do, not because of our faith that "God is with us." In being the hands and feet of God, we make God's reality our reality. Thus, true faith requires believing that what we do makes a difference and that ultimately we help make sure, as Martin Luther King Jr. was fond of saying, "the arc of history bends toward justice." In communal prayer, we are reminded that the values of our tradition, not the marketplace, provide our lodestar for redemption and that we are not alone in our struggle for meaning and purpose in life. Our ancestors struggled as well and somehow made their way; they left us a road map, a spiritual guide, in the prayers of the siddur. In communal prayer, we move both backward and forward in time, honoring and celebrating the past, while reaching out toward the promise of the future.

3

In Genesis we are told that all *b'nei adam* (בְּנֵי אָדָם), "earthlings," are created *b'tzelem Elohim* (בְּצֶלֶם אֱלֹהִים), "in God's image." Yet during the revelation at Mount Sinai, God says to Moses that if *B'nei Yisrael* (בְּנֵי יִשְׂרָאֵל), "the Israelites," follow God's commandments, they will be "a special treasure to Me above all people . . . a kingdom of priests and a holy nation" (Exodus 19:5–6). This tension between the particular and the universal evident in Torah deepens in Rabbinic literature.

Jewish tradition greets the concept of "chosenness" with ambivalence. Yet, our tradition never rejected the idea altogether. If nothing else, "chosenness" was a hopeful light at the end of the dark tunnel of Jewish history. Israel would bear the burden of its special place in God's plan knowing that someday God would make good on God's word. We would be as we were promised, an *am s'gulah* (עַם סְגֻלָּה), "God's treasured people" (Deuteronomy 14:1–2). (I prefer the teaching of Rabbi

Chanan Brichto, *z"l*, whom I heard say once that "anyone is chosen if he chooses to live a holy life.")

Jews "go messianic" when life is so harsh that our only hope seems to depend on divine intervention on a grand scale. Messianism, in all its forms, serves as an antidote to despair over the human condition. The fantastic rise of science and the Industrial Revolution offered the illusion that we could solve all our problems and create heaven on earth; human advances could lead to near perfection of the world. But by the mid-twentieth century, two world wars, the Shoah, and the threat of atomic annihilation shattered the illusion of infinite progress.

If I lean toward messianism at all today, it is to pray, cry out, and beg for God to enter history again, with the "mighty hand" and "outstretched arm" of our mythic past (Deuteronomy 7:19), to free us from the Egypts of our age and take us—all of humanity—home in the full sense of the word: *Bayom hahu yih'yeh Adonai echad ush'mo echad* (בַּיּוֹם הַהוּא יִהְיֶה יְיָ אֶחָד וּשְׁמוֹ אֶחָד), on that day, *Adonai* will be one, and God's name will be one (Zechariah 14:9).

4

Any obligation Jews might feel to enter into dialogue with members of other faith communities arises from our liberalism and not from traditional Judaism. To be sure, there has always been a concern from within the tradition *mipnei darchei shalom* (מִפְּנֵי דַּרְכֵי שָׁלוֹם), which literally means "because of the ways of peace" but is better understood in this context as "for good relations with the gentiles." For example, the Talmud teaches that Jews should "feed non-Jewish poor together with Jewish poor, visit their sick together with Jewish sick people," not because it is our moral obligation, but rather *mipnei darchei shalom*, "because of the ways of peace," that is, to foster good relations with the non-Jewish world (*Mishnah Gittin* 5:8). I share our tradition's concern for *darchei shalom*; ignorance breeds hatred, and thus good relations with the gentiles is usually fostered by interfaith dialogue.

Nevertheless, a desire to get along with our gentile neighbors does not add up to an obligation. My desire for interfaith fellowship and discourse comes not from a sense of obligation, but from my commitment to pluralism and my belief that God is most present in the space in between people when they meet each other as "thou," manifestations of the Divine. Some of my most profound religious experiences have arisen from interfaith dialogue when we approach each other from a place of respect and intense interest. In addition, nothing clarifies my own beliefs more than encounters with other faith traditions or belief systems.

RABBI JEFFREY W. GOLDWASSER

1

> Scripture teaches, "The Tablets were the work of God and the writing was the work of God, *charut* (חָרוּת), "engraved," upon the Tablets" (Exodus 32:16). Do not read *charut*, but rather *cheirut* (חֵרוּת), "freedom," for there is no one who is truly free who does not engage in the study of Torah.
>
> —*Pirkei Avot* 6:2

The rabbis who wrote this teaching wanted us to see a paradox. The Torah and its commandments bind us to laws that have been imposed upon us, yet our greatest freedom comes from the acceptance of Torah. As human beings, we learn that our bodies and souls are filled with all kinds of needs and desires but that not everything we want is good for us. The freedom to pursue all our appetites is actually a form of slavery. Real freedom comes from choosing to engage in a discipline and an order that helps us find mastery over ourselves and fulfillment of our highest aspirations. Judaism teaches us to become the champions of our own lives.

Viewed this way, autonomy is not a new idea introduced into Judaism by the modern age. Judaism depends on our ability to choose and accept Torah. God has no need for automatons. The covenant is a relationship with God in which we willingly espouse a path that leads us toward the joy of service to others, community, purposeful living, and spiritual fulfillment.

Our relationship with God is one of love. In a relationship between human lovers, relationship means freely choosing to be constrained by the needs of the one we love. In the same way, Torah and mitzvot emerge from our loving relationship with God. However, also as in a loving relationship with a person, our relationship with God cannot be one-sided. We respond to God by accepting the right and the obligation to help shape the terms of the relationship in a way that serves our needs, too.

Our part of the *b'rit* (בְּרִית), "covenant," is to engage with the mitzvot lovingly. We have the right to question the ways of the tradition that we find harmful to our being. Just as Rabbinic Judaism has done since ancient times, we have an obligation to alter the tradition to meet the needs of our times. We accept, we choose, we shape, we lovingly find ways to turn our will toward God's will and, in so doing, we discover freedom.

2

Have you ever noticed how liberal Jews rarely, if ever, define themselves as "religious"? Even people who dutifully send their children to religious school, support the synagogue financially, participate in worship services, and observe the holidays tend to think of "religious Jews" as being somebody else. It would be a terrible indictment of liberal Judaism if not even its own most active adherents believed themselves to be "religious." But we know why liberal Jews avoid that label.

Like a candidate being outspent in an election campaign, liberal Jews often allow themselves to be defined by their opponents. We have accepted the idea that "being religious" means being Orthodox, so we have abandoned the term. We do not need to do that.

From the standpoint of traditional Judaism, being "religious" does not mean being more observant than others. It does not mean believing in specific doctrines. The classical Rabbinic Hebrew terms that most closely approximate the English phrase "being religious" all have to do with a person's inner experience, not outer adherence to an Orthodox practice or a standard set of beliefs.

A religious and faithful Jew is one who lives in *yirat shamayim* (יִרְאַת שָׁמַיִם), "Reverence for Heaven," and *ahavat HaShem* (אַהֲבַת הַשֵּׁם), "Love of God." A faithful Jew is one whose deepest loyalty is in the eternal values of our tradition and one who finds greatest fulfillment in a connection to the source of our being.

There are things we do to affirm that internal experience through external action. One of the most obvious is prayer.

When we pray, we attempt to put our experience of life's ultimate meaning into words. The only prayer that cannot work is one that is made with an empty heart. As our tradition teaches, "If a person makes prayer a merely rote recitation, it is not a true entreaty to God" (*Mishnah B'rachot* 4:4).

In Jewish tradition, the ideal way to pray is with others. The experience of praying together reminds us that our relationship to God is communal. By connecting to God as a community, we rediscover that being "religious" is something that we can all share, regardless of our individual choices, beliefs, and observance.

3

Our relationship with God is described as a *b'rit* that binds us to God with commitments and expectations. Being in covenant with God does not preclude other people from having their own sacred connection, but it does mean that our relationship is specific and communal. We, as Jews, believe that we have accepted a unique call to action that emerges from our relationship with God.

We are a people committed to bringing justice into the world. We listen to the voices of our prophets that tell us, "Do what is just and right. Rescue from the defrauder the one who has been robbed. Do no wrong to the stranger, the fatherless and the widow" (Jeremiah 22:3). We are charged with being "a light unto the nations" (Isaiah 49:6).

God's role in this mutual covenant is to bring redemption into the world. We hold God to the promise that the world and humanity will, some day, be "very good," as God declared us to be in the act of Creation (Genesis 1:31). Clearly, we are not there yet. We believe in the hope that together with God, we can repair the brokenness of our world.

The idea often is expressed in Jewish tradition as the hope for *Mashiach* (מָשִׁיחַ), "the anointed Messiah," who will herald *haolam haba* (הָעוֹלָם הַבָּא), "the world-to-come," an existence beyond death. We include this idea in our prayers metaphorically when we praise God for "keeping faith with those who sleep in the dust" (siddur, *G'vurot* blessing of the Amidah).

As liberal Jews, we do not accept a literal belief in a human Messiah who will redeem the world and presage the resurrection of the dead. We reject it not just because of its supernatural expectations, but, more importantly, because it cheapens the deeper meaning of *haolam haba*, turning it into a faraway fantasy world. The verb *haba* is in the present tense. We see "the world-to-come" as something we can access in the here and now.

We discover our redemption whenever we transcend our limitations and overcome our flaws. Our physical existence in this world may end, but our life in the eyes of God is forever. Lives lived meaningfully never really end. They continue to leave a lasting impression upon the universe. We can become our own Messiah by discovering ourselves to be creatures touched by divinity.

4

Hillel taught, "Do not separate yourself from the community" (*Pirkei Avot* 2:5). For most of Jewish history, that was a call for Jews to stick by one another in mutual care and support. In our contemporary reality, though, where we live close by others on a more crowded and complex planet, the teaching is rightly expanded beyond the Jewish community. We separate ourselves from dialogue and fellowship with other faith groups only to our own peril.

Interfaith dialogue helps us to break down walls of misunderstanding and mistrust. When we build bridges of understanding with members of other faith groups, we receive a double benefit. First, we help dispel the stereotypes and animosity upon which anti-Jewish sentiment feeds. We enhance our own security and open doors of acceptance in the larger community. Second, building bridges to other faith groups helps us build a Jewish community that makes choices based on real knowledge and understanding of others, not on our own fears and stereotypes.

When we take the time to get to know and understand the people we might otherwise distrust—a list that might include evangelical Christians, Muslims, Sikhs, Humanists, and Bahá'ís—we pursue both our practical and our spiritual goals. We become better equipped to participate effectively in our communities, and we heal the brokenness we experience when we make ourselves prisoners of fear and hatred.

Judaism has nothing to fear from contact with other faiths. If we are secure and confident in our beliefs, we can only gain from learning about the beliefs of others. What is more, learning together with people who hallow some of our own sacred texts—especially Christians and Muslims—can help us understand our own faith more deeply and confront questions that would not have arisen otherwise.

RABBI AMMIEL HIRSCH

1

Jews are a people.

This founding principle was already established at our earliest moments: "I will make of you a great nation, and I will bless you" (Genesis 12:2–3). "You shall be to Me a kingdom of priests and a holy nation" (Exodus 19:6). "I created you and appointed you a covenant people" (Isaiah 42:6).

The entire people experienced revelation. No other faith makes such a claim. "And if you ask what was it like when the people stood at Sinai hearing God's voice, the answer will be 'Like no other event in the history of man.' There are countless legends, myths, reports, but none of them tells of a whole people witnessing an event such as Sinai" (Abraham Joshua Heschel, *God in Search of Man*, 189).

And thus, already at the beginning of Judaism, there is created a *b'rit* (בְּרִית), "special bond," between our people and God and among Jews themselves. This covenant is both contemporaneous—we are bound in special ways to all Jews living today—and also a covenant of the ages that connects us to all Jews who ever lived and will one day live after us:

> You stand this day, all of you, before the Eternal your God . . . to enter into the covenant . . . that God is concluding with you this

> day . . . in order to establish you this day as God's people. . . . I make this covenant . . . not with you alone, but both with those who are standing here with us this day . . . and with those who are not with us here this day. (Deuteronomy 29:9–14)

The Bible—indeed, the entire subsequent annals of Jewish history—are essentially the record of this covenant in action. Thus, as liberal Jews, the concepts of "autonomy," "covenant," and "commandment" must themselves be understood in this unique Jewish way. Autonomy must have boundaries; it must have room for and serve the broader framework of the covenant of the Jewish people. We do not seek unfettered autonomy. Rather, we aspire to maximal personal and institutional autonomy limited by and serving the needs of the Jewish people. The principal framework is the Jewish people, not the individual Jew or the local synagogue or the national movement.

The concept of mitzvah must include obligations to the Jewish people. Of course we value individuality—much of Judaism teaches the special dignity and standing of the individual created in God's image. And of course we value communal autonomy—throughout the postexilic period, the authority of the local community to determine Jewish practice was emphasized and prized. But these are not ends in and of themselves; they are necessary ingredients to advance the most central—and sacred—principle: the integrity, vitality, and continuity of the Jewish people.

2

Judaism is the faith of the Jewish people.

While "being religious" and "having faith" are critical components of Jewish civilization, these are not, nor have they ever been, the determining factors of Jewishness. Unlike Christianity, Jewish status is not determined by what we believe.

Naturally, millennia of Jewish history have produced a universe of principles and beliefs that we describe as "Jewish," but according to the traditional Rabbinic approach, once we have acquired Jewish status, whether by birth or conversion, we do not cease being Jewish even if we no longer profess belief. Jews may or may not believe in God, *b'rit*, or mitzvah; they may even express beliefs that are outside broadly accepted Jewish parameters. They are still Jews.

While the principle of Jewish peoplehood is itself religious, it is broad enough to include a nonreligious worldview as well. Many Jews do not consider themselves religious but nonetheless claim a strong Jewish identity and attachment to the Jewish people. Their Jewish status is not questioned even by the most religious Jews.

Religious action must follow religious principle accordingly. When it comes to communal prayer, for example, the language of the Jewish people—Hebrew—should be emphasized. The ritual garb of the Jewish people—*kippot*, *tallitot*—should be encouraged. The music of the Jewish people—Jewish-sounding and traditionally rooted musical themes—should be employed.

In mode and mood, the feel of communal prayer should be Jewish. The prayers themselves should include particularistic Jewish aspirations: "We praise the Master of All . . . who has made us different from all the other nations" (*Aleinu*). The Land of Israel (*Eretz Yisrael*, אֶרֶץ יִשְׂרָאֵל) and the State of Israel (*M'dinat Yisrael*, מְדִינַת יִשְׂרָאֵל) should have newly interpreted theological prominence in our liturgy. Prayers referring to the ingathering of the exiles should be expressed.

Broad communal participation should be our goal. The purpose of communal prayer is not only the worship of God; there should also be room for "nonreligious," "secular," or "cultural" Jews to experience communal solidarity that inspires and strengthens their sense of belonging to the Jewish people. Even if these Jews do not consider prayer to be a religious experience, religious Jews would still see a religious purpose that is being served: the strengthening of *K'lal Yisrael* (כְּלָל יִשְׂרָאֵל), "the community of Israel."

3

Does the Jewish people, *qua* people, have a unique vocation among the nations?

This question has always been at the heart of Reform Judaism. From the founding of Reform Judaism in nineteenth-century Germany, there has been a persistent push away from Jewish "ethnicity" toward the pull of universal brotherhood. "The people of Israel no longer lives . . . it has been transformed into a community of faith" (Abraham Geiger, quoted in R. Hirsch, *From the Hill to the Mount*, 160). The mission of Reform Judaism is "to transform the national Jew into a religious Jew" (Kohler, *Jewish Theology*, 391). "We consider ourselves no longer a nation but a religious community" (CCAR, Pittsburgh Platform, 1885).

The twentieth-century genocide of European Jewry, perpetrated by Germany, itself demonstrated that, as critics of Reform Judaism always contended, these messianic expectations of "universal brotherhood [were] not even a beautiful dream" (Theodore Herzl, quoted in Ellenson, "Reform Zionism Today," 13). The perpetrators of the Shoah didn't care what individual Jews believed; they sought the elimination of the Jewish people.

And thus, late twentieth-century Reform Jews returned to the centrality of Jewish peoplehood and even embraced the very Zionism that was so antithetical to the Reform Judaism of the past: "The restoration of *Am Yisrael* to its ancestral homeland . . . represents an historic triumph of the Jewish people . . . and the realization of God's promise to Abraham" (CCAR, Miami Platform, 1997).

Our task today is to insist on the traditional Jewish understanding of universalism, a unique blend of universal aims through particular means. Judaism's concern is with the particular—the Jewish people—that practices a universal purpose: to "do what is right and just" (Genesis 18:19), to "repair the world under the sovereignty of God" (siddur), to be "a light to the nations, opening eyes deprived of light" (Isaiah 42:6–7).

We believe in universal goals; we aspire to a messianic era of peace, but we assert that the way to achieve these goals is not through the abandonment of communal bonds, but on the contrary, universalism is best achieved through collectivities. Peoples are the key actors of history, not individuals. And history itself, in Jewish thought, is the medium through which messianic aspirations will be achieved. The forces of history—politics and policies—and not an individual savior will one day produce an era of peace and tranquility, when "all shall sit under vine and fig tree and none shall be afraid" (Micah 4:4).

4

In order to achieve these universal goals of peace and tranquility—or even simply to try and make the world a little bit better—we must work with anyone and everyone who is willing to advance these aims. The world is so broken by religious conflict that it is a fundamental moral imperative to help repair this brokenness, to engage in *tikkun* (תִּיקוּן), to alleviate poverty and despair, to encourage diversity and equality.

It is not only desirable, but we have an obligation to partner with forces from the Christian and Muslim communities. These faith communities are much larger than the Jewish people and can contribute so much to a more just, prosperous, and peaceful world.

In this realm, too, the centrality of Jewish peoplehood should be upheld. We should see ourselves as advocates for Israel. We should consider ourselves representatives and guardians of the Jewish people. Nothing can dilute our commitment to distinctive Jewish existence:

For us Jews there can be no fellowship with God without the fellowship with the people Israel. Abandoning Israel, we desert God. . . . What we do as individuals is a trivial episode; what we attain as Israel causes us to grow into the infinite. (Heschel, *God in Search of Man*, 423)

RABBI BRUCE KADDEN

1

As a Reform Jew, I affirm that the *b'rit* (בְּרִית), "covenant," that God first made with Abraham (Genesis 12) and extended to the entire people Israel at Mount Sinai (Exodus 19–20) continues to define my relationship to the Jewish people and the relationship of the Jewish people to God. When I affirm that I am part of this covenant, I commit myself to supporting *K'lal Yisrael* (כְּלָל יִשְׂרָאֵל), "the greater community of Israel," which also embraces this covenant. I also commit myself to maintaining a relationship with the Divine through study and wrestling with Torah.

The Torah is sacred because it was created through our earliest ancestors' encounters with the Divine and with each other. Their experiences were passed on orally until written down and reshaped over a number of generations, before taking form as the text we read today. Through studying the written Torah in subsequent generations, our people has produced an Oral Torah, which attempts to understand and apply the teachings of the text in an ever-changing Jewish world. This Oral Torah includes Mishnah and Talmud, midrash, responsa, commentaries, and codes of law, but also philosophical works, poetry, novels, and our own discussions that draw their inspiration from the text.

The Torah is the primary source for mitzvot (sacred obligations). By wrestling with Torah and its interpretations throughout the ages, we come to understand that some mitzvot are incumbent upon all human beings (the Noahide Laws), and some mitzvot are incumbent on every Jew (such as studying Torah, visiting the sick, and observing Shabbat). In addition, each person will determine how to fulfill the mitzvot he or she finds compelling and meaningful as an individual, a member of a family, and/or a member of a Jewish community.

Many of these mitzvot have been observed by our people throughout the ages. Other mitzvot may be contemporary interpretations of classical mitzvot. Still other mitzvot may be radically new observances or obligations that we derive through studying Torah and creating communities with our fellow Jews. As we continue to wrestle with Torah, our understanding of the *b'rit* and mitzvot evolves. Through this process, we together create the Judaism of today and tomorrow.

2

I am a religious Jew.

A religious Jew wrestles with Torah to understand how to live one's life. A religious Jew engages in acts of *tzedakah* (צְדָקָה), "justice," and *tikkun olam* (תִּיקּוּן עוֹלָם), "repairing the world," and understands such acts as one's personal response to Torah.

A religious Jew leads a prayerful life both individually and as part of a community.

A religious Jew participates with God in the ongoing process of Creation.

A religious Jew is part of a Jewish community, affirming a responsibility for sharing joys and difficult times with one another.

A religious Jew affirms a connection to *K'lal Yisrael* (כְּלָל יִשְׂרָאֵל), "the greater Jewish community," and supports Jews in need around the world.

A religious Jew affirms the centrality of the State of Israel as *reishit tz'michat g'ulateinu* (רֵאשִׁית צְמִיחַת גְּאֻלָּתֵנוּ), "the beginning sprout of redemption," and supports Israel through words and deeds.

A religious Jew wrestles with God, the meaning of life and death, the reality of evil, and other ultimate human questions.

A religious Jew is not defined by dress, dietary habits, or frequency of service attendance. Rather, a religious Jew is defined by a commitment to wrestling with God, studying Torah, engaging in acts of *g'milut chasadim* (גְּמִילוּת חֲסָדִים), "loving-kindness," and loving Israel (the people and the state).

A religious Jew affirms hope in the messianic age, a time of peace and justice envisioned by the prophets, and commits to the realization of that vision.

A religious Jew accepts the realities of evil, pain, and suffering but maintains faith that these realities can be transformed into opportunities for growth and goodness through love from God and from one's fellow human beings.

Some religious Jews have fully embraced the beliefs and traditions that they inherited. Other religious Jews have challenged and significantly altered those beliefs and traditions, creating new ways to be Jewish. What all these religious Jews have in common is a love of God, Torah, and the Jewish people and a commitment to passing on a vibrant and meaningful Judaism to the next generation.

3

"A Statement of Principles for Reform Judaism," adopted by the Central Conference of American Rabbis in 1999, affirmed: "We are Israel, a people aspiring to holiness, singled out through our ancient covenant and our unique history among the nations to be witnesses to God's presence" (CCAR, A Statement of Principles for Reform Judaism). This statement affirms two aspects of our unique vocation.

First of all, we are to aspire to holiness, responding to God's charge in Leviticus, "You shall be holy, for I, the Eternal your God, am holy" (19:2). To be holy means to be set apart or unique. We are the only people for whom the Torah is the foundation of our religion. All authentic Jewish teaching derives from Torah and our wrestling with it. Through this process, we strive to become a holy people, fully manifesting God's teachings in our words and deeds.

Secondly, we are called upon to be witnesses to God's presence, or in the words of the prophet Isaiah, to be "a light to the nations" (49:6). Rabbi Harold Kushner explains that to be a light to the nations means that the Jewish people "were to be a 'pilot project,' a demonstration community. God would give them explicit instructions about how to carry on the God-centered life. If they did it . . . they would bring the other peoples of the world to see how satisfying it is to live that way" (*To Life!*, 31). The "explicit instructions" are, of course, our Torah. Our ongoing wrestling with Torah helps us to live our lives in service to God and to our fellow human beings. We hope that as others observe us, they will be inspired to explore their own relationship with the Divine, either through another religion that worships God or through the exploration and embrace of Judaism.

Our people has always looked toward the future. When our ancestors were wandering in the wilderness of Sinai, they looked toward settling in the Promised Land. After settling in the Land, they looked toward uniting the tribes and building the Temple. After the destruction of the Temple and exile, they looked forward to return and rebuilding.

The prophets of Israel envisioned a messianic age, a world of peace and justice, of love and caring for one another. Reform Judaism has embraced this vision and affirmed that each of us should work toward realizing this vision through *tikkun olam*.

4

At times in Jewish history there was little opportunity for any meaningful interfaith dialogue. Conflict and disputation were sometimes the hallmark of Jewish and Christian contact, though there were relations that demonstrated understanding and serious discussion. In the Middle Ages, Jews and Muslims enjoyed extensive and fruitful dialogue.

The Second Vatican Council, particularly the document known as *Nostra Aetate*, "In Our Time," revolutionized interfaith relations following its publication in 1965. *Nostra Aetate* affirmed the unity of the origin of all human beings, as well as religious truths that are found in many religious traditions. It also acknowledged the bonds that tie Christianity to Judaism through our common ancestor, Abraham. Finally, this declaration rejected the charge of deicide and all displays of contemporary anti-Semitism. Not only did *Nostra Aetate* lead to much improved Jewish-Catholic relations, but it also influenced other Christian denominations to reexamine their relationships with Judaism and created a climate where dialogue and cooperation have become the norm in our time.

We Jews should therefore welcome the opportunity to engage in meaningful interfaith dialogue with Christians, Muslims, Buddhists, and other religious communities. The purpose of such dialogue is to share openly and honestly beliefs and practices of our religious traditions, appreciating those things we have in common and acknowledging our differences. Such dialogue not only helps us better understand our neighbors and their religions, but also better appreciate and understand Judaism.

Our dialogues might include studying Scripture together, to better understand how each religion interprets biblical stories and teachings and how such interpretations influence the way we practice our religion. The dialogues might also include comparing how we understand important religious terms and values such as *tzedakah*/charity/*zakat* (Islam's pillar of charitable giving); peace/*shalom*/*salaam*; messiah and redemption; sin, repentance, and forgiveness, and so on.

Such dialogue can often lead to recognizing shared values and the opportunity to work with one another to promote such values as peace and justice in our communities. We can work together to provide housing for the homeless, food for the hungry, and clothing and goods for those in need, or to pursue peace and justice on a national or international scale. Working together with other religious communities demonstrates a common commitment to core religious values without compromising the beliefs and traditions that make us unique.

RABBI RACHEL S. MIKVA

1

Covenant and Commandment

Intimacy breeds high expectations. It does not matter whether the foundation of our Jewish relationship is a theistic concept of God, an abiding connection with Jewish history and culture, or nurturing a Jewish home; we internalize the claims made on us as mitzvah. As with our other covenantal relationships—as spouses, parents, and children—we know that we will often fall short and still the bond abides. We also know, however, that the relationship grows richer each time we can respond with the fullness of our being: *hineini* (הִנֵּנִי), "here I am."

Torah

The stumbling block to viewing Torah as a sacred text is not that God didn't write it; it is that the humans who wrote it left us such a problematic legacy. Genocide and slavery, patriarchy and homophobia, superstition and family dysfunction—*this* is Scripture? Sure, there are many inspiring passages—a vision of a nation that tends to the poor and the stranger, a Creation in Genesis 1 that imagines gender equality, a narrative that has inspired the Western world with ideas of freedom, and prophets who call us to account for our moral failings. But what is all that other junk doing there?

As Yehudah Amichai recounts in his poem "*HaZeman*":

> I've filtered out of the Book of Esther
> the residue of vulgar joy, and out of the Book of Jeremiah
> the howl of pain in the guts. And out of the
> Song of Songs the endless search
> for love, and out of the Book of Genesis
> the dreams and Cain, and out of Ecclesiastes
> the despair and out of the Book of Job—Job.
> And from what was left over I pasted for myself a new Bible.
> Now I live censored and pasted and limited and in peace . . . .

What is he saying? Basically, he took out everything that was ethically objectionable, emotionally unbearable, or intellectually suspect—and there wasn't much left. The power and sanctity of Torah are uncovered precisely in digging through the rough parts. My teacher Rabbi Arnold Jacob Wolf used to say that Scripture is not a boy scout manual. It is not to be read as a guidebook with all the answers. It has the *questions*. Torah is a syllabus for a lifelong course in advanced ethics.

Contradictions within the text, a multiplicity of interpretations, clash with contemporary values—all these irritants are designed to create dialectical tension. We read closely, consider carefully, consult history, rub the sore spots—and we produce from the bothersome grains of sand precious pearls of scriptural instruction. We cannot simply spiritualize or ignore the painful passages because that is where the ethical work really happens—texts as tools of moral development.

2

When I was a congregational rabbi, I used to take fifth graders and their families away on retreat in the spring. Frequently the weekly Torah reading was *K'doshim* (קְדוֹשִׁים), which contains the charge "You shall be holy, for I, *YHVH* your God, am holy" (Leviticus 19:2)—and before we read the text, I asked participants to describe a holy person. Invariably, they responded with models they knew from Christian contexts: monastics who leave mainstream society to live out their days in prayer and contemplation or who dedicate themselves to lives of poverty in their service to the suffering. After reading parts of Leviticus 19, however, they revised their portrait: ordinary people who honor their parents, make Shabbat, generously share their blessings, are scrupulous in business, model profound integrity and a capacity for forgiveness, are careful not to speak ill of others, guard the rights of the laborer and the stranger, and so forth.

Torah transformed their expectations by offering a model of Jewish religiosity that invests the details of our daily lives with the potential for holiness. Most important is the idea that the person of faith is not "someone else," not the person who does religion professionally, not the more observant Jew, not the evangelical Christian who talks about God all the time—but you.

Ritual and ethical in form, conscious and unconscious in execution, every time you respond to the call of the covenant you are a person of faith. In theory, it does not require communal prayer any more than other avenues of response. But I can tell you this: I struggled with finding a spiritual home once I entered academia, so after twenty years of a regular prayer life, I now daven relatively infrequently. I still study sacred texts and teach them in religious contexts; I still observe Shabbat and festivals, keep kosher, and work for social justice; I still try with every decision I make to become the human being God created me to be. But my relationship with God and with the Jewish community, my capacities for critique of self and empathy for others, the depth of my *kavanah* (כַּוָּנָה), "intention," and my commitment—all have become attenuated. Communal prayer is the spiritual discipline that develops religious muscles and sharpens the vision of faith.

3

Another world is possible. I affirm Rabbi Jonathan Sacks's insight that "faith is not acceptance but protest, against the world that is, in the name of the world that is not yet but ought to be" (*To Heal a Fractured World*, 27). To the extent that the mythology of a messianic age inspires work to alleviate poverty and oppression, violence and violation, I believe. I affirm religious ideas that give hope in a broken world and catalyze efforts for its repair—even if we never get "there." As Danny Siegel adapted from a Yiddish proverb, "If you always assume the person sitting next to you is the Messiah, waiting for some simple human kindness, you will soon come to weigh your words and watch your hands. And if he chooses not to be revealed in your time, it will not matter" (Siegel, *And God Braided Eve's Hair*).

Does the Jewish people have some special role in this endeavor? Mordecai Kaplan suggested the concept of vocation as a substitute for the dangerous arrogance of chosenness and the religious imperialism of mission. As an obviously *human* construct, vocation guards against the insidious notion that God plays favorites or that sacred purpose might be the monopoly of any one people. We have heard the divine call in a unique and essential way, as have other religious traditions. Each path has the capacity to inspire its adherents with faith in the importance of their work, and God has an enduring stake in our embodiment of the teaching, making the covenant(s) real and reciprocal. There is no scarcity in chosenness, because God does not cease to "choose," calling us to respond. In fact, God never shuts up.

Yes, Jews have a unique vocation, profoundly bound up with living and learning Torah. Even the idea of vocation is fraught, however, open to perilous transformation of a sacred task into destiny, obligation into prerogative. *Tanach* (תנ"ך), "the Hebrew Bible," cautions us against such contortions. Although Genesis is replete with insight about the conundrum of divinely sanctioned destiny—Cain's murderous rage at being unchosen, Jacob's duplicity in capturing the birthright and blessing, and so on—it is the Joseph novella that is perhaps most instructive for our current purposes.

Joseph is certain of his unique role in the story of redemption, and it breeds resentment among the brothers. It is only in their mutual recognition of "vocation" that the divine plan for blessing can unfold. The covenantal promise is, for the first time, transmitted to all the siblings, and they become embedded in relationships of reciprocal dependence with each other and with the Egyptians. Blessing flows between and among the households of Creation. The vision of Isaiah is similar: "In that day, Israel shall be a third partner with Egypt and Assyria as a blessing on earth; for *YHVH* of Hosts will bless them saying: Blessed be My people Egypt, My handiwork Assyria, and My legacy Israel (19:24–25). We only get there together.

4

So far, this century is most notable for the resurgence of religion as the primary paradigm for resorting to violence against others—even if it is frequently a front for conflicts more fundamentally driven by competition for power and resources. Interfaith and intra-faith engagement is imperative, with mutual respect that grows from knowledge. (Unfortunately, we don't know enough even about the varieties of Judaism, especially communities of colors other than white, e.g., the Abayudaya, Lemba, Ibo, Bene Israel, Beta Israel, and Ethiopian Hebrew communities.)

In pursuit of understanding, deep encounter, and collective work toward the common good, deep learning about diverse religious traditions is now a civic responsibility. Activism is also required. We need interreligious leaders (not only clergy), people who organize "Read the Qur'an Day" in response to those who threatened "Burn the Qur'an Day," people who build bridges over chasms of ignorance and fear.

Learning with and about the other, we also deepen our understanding of our own faith. Identity is a construction built in conversation and comparison. As iron sharpens iron, so one person sharpens the countenance of his neighbor (Proverbs 27:17). We refract other traditions through the lens of our own: How might Hindu-goddess worship help us understand what it means to engender God (as either male or female)? How do stories of Muslims in America illuminate our own negotiation of acculturation and Jewish distinctiveness? One reading unsettles another, engages it, refines it—and as a result, we will never be the same. Of course, we cannot erase the independent value of the other in pursuit of self-understanding. No respectful encounter can be "all about me," even if it demonstrates a readiness to be changed by the meeting.

What do Jews carry into dialogue? We bear Moses's experience in the cleft of the rock, aware that we cannot see the "face" of God (Exodus 33:18–23). God meets us in our finitude; to hear the word of God in human terms cannot help but be a diminution and distortion to some degree. We bear the theophany at Sinai: "I *YHVH* am your God who took you out of the land of Egypt" (Exodus 20:2)—not principles of monotheism but a particular relationship—the story of one people with its God, eager to hear others. We bring the Rabbinic emphasis on hospitality, embrace of multivocality, and valorization of humility. We bear witness through Jewish history that humanity must learn to celebrate difference, not eliminate it.

RABBI EVAN MOFFIC

1

Covenant is the sustaining idea of Jewish life. It connotes a sacred relationship, a commitment between God and the Jewish people. It began with Abraham. It was affirmed by Moses in the Exodus from Egypt. And it was sealed with the entire people through the giving and acceptance of the Torah at Mount Sinai. It is sustained through the practice of mitzvot. To live by the covenant is to make the Torah sacred and to make ourselves and our community sacred.

Yet, sacred does not mean frozen. The covenant is dynamic. It is not fixed by one time and place. It is rooted in the past, yet evolves into the future. We are meant to hear the word of God in the present tense. We are meant to listen for its message for our time. Martin Buber expressed this as follows: "The eternal revelation is here and now. I do not believe in a self-definition of God prior to the experience of human beings. . . . The eternal voice of strength flows, the eternal voice sounds forth to us now" (Buber, *I and Thou*, 84–85).

Buber's conception may sound mystical, but it is also eminently practical and relevant for us today. Rabbi Jonathan Sacks paints a picture of what Buber's conception means in action in a beautiful story about an encounter he had. Rabbi Sacks was the chief rabbi of Great Britain from 1990 to 2013, and his work included several cutting-edge questions of medical ethics. In this capacity, he met with Lord Robert

Winston, one of the world's leading researchers on in vitro fertilization, embryo development, and the human genome.

During their visit in Lord Winston's office, Sacks noticed a copy of the Five Books of Moses, wedged between volumes of the latest scientific research. In addition, several volumes of commentary, along with a prayer book, sat near them. Even though he is a cutting-edge scientist pushing the boundaries of life, Lord Winston is a deeply religious man whose faith guides him in the critical work he does. For him, the covenant is ongoing, continuing to guide his work and values.

So it is with us. We do not live *in* the past. Rather, we live *with* the past, drawing from the accumulated wisdom of our tradition in order to build a better future. We see our lives as part of a journey that began before us, continues after us, and is carried forward by and through us. That is what it means to be part of a covenant.

2

In Judaism, it does not make sense to say, "I have faith in God." Rather, it makes sense to say, "I live with faithfulness to God." Judaism is not a set of propositions. It is a way of life. To be religious is to follow, as best one can, the way of life set forth in the Torah and lived by hundreds of generations of the Jewish people.

Prayer is one of the ways we live out the Jewish way of life. First, it is a statement of principles. Reciting the Pledge of Allegiance or singing the national anthem is a way we express a dedication to American ideals. Similarly, praying is a way we express a commitment to Jewish tradition. Second, it is a concrete way of expressing our faithfulness to the Jewish way of life. We pray not only to find comfort. We pray not only to express gratitude. We pray because it is part of the definition of Jewish living set forth in Torah and Jewish tradition. This approach to prayer helps us understand why it is imperative to pray as part of a community. We cannot be Jewish all alone.

Consider this teaching from Maimonides: "The prayer of the community is always heard. . . . Hence a person must join with the community, and should not pray alone so long as one is able to pray with the community" (*Mishneh Torah*, Laws of Prayer 8:1).

This may seem rather strange at first. Why should God care whether a person is praying alone or as part of a larger group? Does the number of people change the nature or content of one's prayer?

My sense is that the number of people may not concern God, but it should concern us. When we worship as part of a larger group, we feel part of something larger. Our words connect us to those around us, helping us understand our interdependence and our responsibility to our community.

Several years ago, Rabbi Larry Kushner wrote a beautiful book called *Invisible Lines of Connection*. When I pray and look around at the community that surrounds me, I imagine all of those invisible lines of connection that link us to one another and to God. Those threads build a holy network and lift each of us a little higher.

3

Asking about a unique vocation for the Jewish people is another way of asking what one believes about the idea of Jews as "the chosen people." I embrace fully the idea that God chose the Jewish people for a unique vocation and role in the world, just as God chose other nations for a unique purpose. The purpose of the Jewish people, as best I can discern it, is to live by and teach the ideals of Torah to the world. These ideals include sexual morality, honoring our ancestors, and the notion, revolutionary in its time, of universal education. To say we are chosen to teach and exemplify these ideals is not to say we have a monopoly on them. It is simply to say they are central to who we are.

It is imperative to state that chosenness does not imply superiority. The best way to convey this idea is to use marriage as a metaphor.

As a husband, I believe my wife is the most beautiful, loving person in the world, and she and I have a unique relationship shared by no one else. At the same time, I believe every married couple has a unique relationship in which they have chosen one another. To say my marriage is superior makes no sense. Similarly, God and the Jewish people have a unique relationship. To say it is superior to the relationship consecrated within other religions does not make sense.

I believe in the coming of a messianic age initiated by God, but I have no idea when it will come to be. The best I can do is to live my life in accordance with the teachings of Torah. The idea of a messianic age gives me faith, however, that I am working for something larger than myself. The problem with social action without faith is that it does not answer the question "What for?" Do we do something good simply because we think it is good? If that's the case, who decides what is good? Yet, when we are working to repair the world, we are guided by a goal and a vision. That vision is a messianic age, a world where, to paraphrase Micah 4:4, "everyone may sit under their vine and fig tree, and none shall make them afraid."

4

I am not sure we are "obligated" to enter into dialogue with members of other faith communities, but I do think dialogue both serves our mission to repair the world and enriches our knowledge of Judaism. Over the years, dialogue with those of other faiths has helped me look more closely at Judaism. When I worked with Christian colleagues in a hospital, for example, I began to explore what Judaism says about spontaneous prayer. When discussing Judaism with Muslim colleagues, I began to focus on what we believe about the afterlife.

I find that even as a rabbi, it is easy to ignore the big questions. We can have Shabbat dinners, lead services, observe the holidays, and still not take the time to engage deeply with the texts and ideas of our tradition. To do so, we need focused time and a desire to study, but we often put it off. We know it is important, but the urgent usually trumps the important. Interfaith dialogue can bring some of those theological questions to the forefront of our minds.

It can also help in our task of repairing the world. We all know that much violence in the world is motivated by religious conviction. We all have friends or acquaintances who wonder whether religion is to blame for all our world's problems. No less a luminary than John Lennon included in his vision of utopia a world with "no religion."

When we converse with those of other faiths—when we share our ideals and our vulnerability, our concerns and our convictions—some of the fear and hostility melt away. If religion is to be a force for peace rather than violence, we must dialogue with each other.

Jews also play a critical educational role in dialogue because we are the oldest of the three monotheisms. Our texts shaped their traditions. When we can communicate the way that happened, we may begin to realize how much we share. We need not paper over our differences, but in a world of limited resources and heightened antagonism, our shared ideals can exert a major influence in reducing violence and enhancing human dignity. Today, more than ever, we have the opportunity to realize the vision of one of the early visionaries of Reform Judaism, Rabbi David Einhorn: "One God over all, and one human family of all" (Einhorn's inaugural address, September 27, 1855).

RABBI JOSEPH A. SKLOOT

1

Adulthood is about acknowledging our capacity to make choices, good and bad, and about accepting the fact that sometimes our choices are limited by outside forces or that sometimes we have no choice at all. Jewish tradition describes the Jewish people's relationship with God similarly. God chose us, the Rabbis say—making us an offer we couldn't refuse—but we also chose God. It's an idea encapsulated in two famous midrashim about the giving of the Torah at Mount Sinai.

In the first midrash, God shops the Torah around, offering it to all the other peoples of the ancient Near East. When they refuse, God offers the Torah to the Israelites in a last-ditch effort. They readily accept it, sight unseen (*Sifrei D'varim*, *V'zot Hab'rachah* 343).

In the second midrash, the Israelites are reluctant to accept the Torah, so God lifts Mount Sinai up off the ground and dangles it above their heads. Under threat of annihilation, the Israelites accept the Torah and all its obligations (Babylonian Talmud, *Shabbat* 88a).

These midrashim should be understood metaphorically. They teach us that Jewishness is a matter of will and fate, autonomy and constraint. From the start, liberal Judaism emphasized the former over the latter. Indebted to Kant, who asserted that genuine piety flowed from an individual's conscious choice, liberal Judaism has taught that all Jews are "Jews by choice." This, to a certain extent, is correct. Today, when there are no state- or community-ordained penalties for non-observance, every ritual we perform, every moment we spend in study, every time we take moral action, we consciously choose to follow the injunctions of tradition.

Yet, liberal Judaism's emphasis on autonomy has obscured the reality that Jewishness is not only a matter of choice. The legacy of generations past continues to shape generations present and future. For the vast majority of us, Jewishness is encoded in our upbringing, our lineage, and even our DNA; and if not, something otherworldly and transcendent calls out to us, reminding us to take our place in the chain of Jewish tradition. I would argue that this force is none other than the commanding voice of God in our lives. While it may seem subtler than violent claps of thunder at Mount Sinai, it is no less powerful. It is the "still small voice" (I Kings 19:12) of destiny that compels us to measure our lives against the ritual and ethical standards enumerated in the Torah, given by God to our people long ago.

2

Judaism is neither a "religion" nor a "faith," in that both terms imply theological commitments. Etymologically, they describe the acknowledgment of and devotion to God or a higher power in the universe. While Judaism certainly *involves* theology, and generations of Jews have speculated about the Holy Blessed One, theology is hardly the sum total of the Jewish experience. The fact that we use these terms to refer to Judaism today is simply a reflection of our adoption of a Christian vocabulary and worldview. From this Christocentric vantage point, Judaism is, like Christianity, primarily about the acceptance of specific theological propositions.

My students routinely demonstrate the inaccuracy of this perspective when I give them a simple assignment: I ask them to brainstorm the characteristics and qualities they associate with "Jewishness." The lists they produce are generally heavy on cultural norms and ritual practices—for example, "learning," "social justice," "synagogue," and "family"—and light on theological concepts. Only after prodding do they cite terms like "covenant" or "monotheism." This discrepancy reflects an essential ambiguity in classical Jewish texts: Jewishness is a complex phenomenon involving a mixture of social, ethnic, ritual, political, psychological, and theological commitments. Compare the works of the philosophers Y'hudah HaLevi and Moses Maimonides: HaLevi conceives of Judaism, first and foremost, as a national entity (e.g., *Kuzari* 1:25–27). Maimonides, by contrast, depicts Judaism as a series of theological commitments (e.g., commentary to *Mishnah Sanhedrin* 10).

Is a person Jewish by accident of her birth or by virtue of the community to which she belongs? Is she a Jew because of the prayers and rituals that fill her life or because of her beliefs about God and God's role in the universe? The answers to these questions will differ depending on whom you ask. The terms "religion" and "faith" are thus ill suited for describing a phenomenon as rich and varied as Judaism.

3

Perhaps Judaism's greatest gift to human culture is an awareness that the present state of world affairs is unsustainable, that human suffering and injustice cannot persist indefinitely, and that there is reason to hope human efforts will one day bring about unending peace. We can trace this insight back to the Exodus, a story at the heart of the Torah and subsequent Jewish tradition. The political philosopher Michael Walzer has famously written that this story "generates a sense of possibility," for without it "oppression would be experienced as an inescapable condition, a matter of personal or collective bad luck, a stroke of fate." Because the chains of injustice were broken once at the Sea of Reeds and the ancient Israelites found their way to their Promised Land, we know a Promised Land awaits us too. Getting there, however, requires constant awareness and effort. "Anger and hope," Walzer writes, "not resignation, are the appropriate responses to the Egyptian house of bondage" in every age (*Exodus and Revolution*, 21–22).

It is all too easy to fall into a posture of resignation in the face of suffering. As custodians of Torah and ongoing witnesses to the inspiring truth of the Exodus narrative, the Jewish people's unique vocation in the world is to goad each other and our neighbors out of complacency. Exodus's call "You shall not wrong nor oppress a stranger, for you were strangers in the land of Egypt" (22:20) and Deuteronomy's command "Remember the day of your departure from the land of Egypt as long as you live" (16:3) form our mission statement. A messianic age awaits us as long as we serve as witnesses to the truth and hope of the Exodus and never abandon our attempts to transform our world into an enduring Promised Land.

4

Too often so-called interfaith dialogue devolves into "show-and-tell" for adults. The conversation begins something like this: "Let's each share something about our Creation stories." The assumed, if unstated, goal is to uncover similarities among venerable traditions. By recognizing how similar we are, the theory goes, we will learn to respect and appreciate one another. But this theory is untenable. Similarity does not necessarily inspire respect or appreciation.

The search for similarity makes today's "interfaith dialogues" both superficial and impersonal. A better approach would be to focus on distinctiveness and difference. Such conversations allow participants to speak far more personally, for they share what matters most to them, what makes them unique and proud. In so doing, they have the potential to foster honest relationships rather than casual conversation. Respect and appreciation are born out of relationship, not merely agreement.

We can learn something about this from Jewish history. Dialogue with non-Jews has been a facet of Jewish life in every era. Yet, these dialogues occurred among people who lived and worked together, sharing in each other's lives by virtue of proximity and economy. Despite or perhaps because of this close contact, our ancestors assumed that Jews were different from Christians and Muslims, radically so, and they assumed those differences were entirely appropriate and beneficial. What differentiates us from others makes us who we are and makes us proud to be who we are.

The informal interfaith dialogues of Jewish history also had an added benefit. In conversation and collaboration with their non-Jewish neighbors, our ancestors learned about new ideas and practices that they then integrated into their own understanding of Judaism—Moses Maimonides's depiction of Jewish civil law reflects the influence of Muslim jurists and their legal codification efforts; the design of a page of Talmud derives from the application of Christian printing conventions to Jewish texts by Jews and Christians working in collaboration. If we assume that we are different from our neighbors and that because of that difference they have something to teach us that we don't already know, we open ourselves up to the possibility of transformation: personal transformation and also the ongoing transformation of Jewish life.

RABBI JOSHUA STANTON

1

Both covenant and commandment rely on history. They are responses on the part of Jews as a group to the significance of their shared history. Derived from the sacred narrative of Torah, they are applied retrospectively to events either that happened in actuality or that Jews adopted as sacred memories, which can feel every bit as real as historical events themselves.

Following the lead of Mordecai Kaplan, I believe that "a people is prior to its religion" (Eugene Borowitz, *Choices in Modern Jewish Thought*, 103). The Jewish people existed before the Torah was given, as is affirmed within the narrative arc of the Torah itself: Abraham was Jewish before Moses went up Mount Sinai. The experiences of the Jewish people existed before they were recast and described within the Torah.

The two concepts of covenant and commandment are significant insofar as they demonstrate the sacred inspiration that exists within people to derive principles from historical narratives. Covenant and commandment shape principles that define the Jews in the present and the future.

What makes the ideas of covenant and commandment significant is the extent to which they manifest the sacred impulse on the part of Jewish human beings to care for the group of which they are a part and take personal responsibility for actions that can contribute to a just society. In relating individual and group, justice and personal accountability, both concepts transcend time and enable Jews to connect to their sacred purpose as people and a people that pursues righteousness.

2

On a trip last year to Vietnam, I became ensconced in an interchange with a nonreligious Spanish engineer about the nature of God. At times it felt more like a debate. At other times, it felt like old friends pursuing truth together ("God as Ordering Force in the Universe," *Huffington Post*, September 9, 2012).

One of the key points of curiosity for the Spanish engineer was why we as human beings matter at all. If we are insignificant as beings, when viewed on a cosmic scale, then why would God care about us?

In some ways, the Spanish engineer evoked an idea made not by a nonreligious person, but by a rabbinic thought-leader, Jeremy Kalmanofsky: "Our narcissistic little species is inclined to view ourselves as protagonists in cosmic dramas of exile and redemption, rebellion and surrender, sin and salvation. We usually fail to absorb what Copernicus proved half a millennium ago: that we do not live at the center of the universe" ("Cosmic Theology and Earthly Religion," 24). This apt point on the part of both my Spanish interlocutor and my rabbinic colleague has furthered my quest to understand what could at once be a force vast enough to be present in the cosmos and yet present in the world in which humans reside.

It has forced me to reconsider the nature of the Torah, God, prayer, and prophecy. Only relatively recently did I find myself able to articulate my views. From a cosmic perspective, it seems unlikely that God would be "personal" and invested in interaction with human beings, but rather would be "abstract" and a Force within the universe. Evidence for God's existence lies not in juxtaposition to scientific inquiry, but precisely because of it: it is uncanny that there is so much order in our universe if (as in the second law of thermodynamics) it should theoretically be devolving and increasing in entropy.

The Ordering Force of the universe that I call God compels us as humans to pursue justice as the highest form of order to which we can aspire. In our own modest way, we connect with the elements of the Force that lies within us and harness it to foster justice in our communities and societies.

The "faith" that inspires us need not be blind or in juxtaposition to science. Rather, it can stem from the paradoxical recognition of both human limitation and our capacity to connect to the Force that transcends time and place.

3

An underlying problem with the idea of particularity is its own universality. Groups and subgroups of people have for millennia defined themselves as somehow chosen or different from all others. As Avi Beker puts it, "Billions of people around the world define their religion, their nation, their tribe, or even their sports teams as the Chosen ones" (*The Chosen*, 1). It is unclear that the idea of "chosenness" remains compelling, at least in the traditional conception.

Even if it were compelling to more contemporary thinkers, it is unclear that chosenness would be desirable. If, for the sake of a thought experiment, we were to presuppose the historical accuracy and sacred origins of the Torah, the exclusivity of God's covenant, if understood in traditional terms, can be uncomfortable for Jews living in an epoch still reeling from bouts of ultra-nationalism and in living memory of communism and fascism in Europe.

With these and other examples in mind, it is inherently problematic to prefer one group over another based on essentialist claims about its identity or historical claims about its sacred designation. Yet the idea of a group identity need not be overlooked entirely so much as reframed. Groups, however they may form, are able to establish and reinforce values among their members. Insofar as the Rabbinic tradition is concerned, in its recasting and reframing of Judaism into the form that self-identified Jews overwhelmingly practice today, the values reinforced clearly inspire the pursuit of justice and ethical comportment. As such, Jews may be seen as choosing themselves or designating themselves for sacred purpose.

In guiding our lives, Rabbinic Judaism and the many elements of Jewish living that have evolved from it have bestowed upon the Jewish people a clear and remarkable purpose. But it is not a process guided by an external God so much as the inspiration that resides within people because of the elements of the Ordering Force of the universe that reside within them. Insofar as this sacred purpose is heightened through group identity and the social mores that it reinforces, the Jews indeed have a singular vocation.

The messianic era, as a symbolic end to the process of creating a truly just society and world, can exist only when the pursuit of justice is reinforced universally, rather than simply within an individual group itself. The role of the Jewish people, paradoxically, may be to transcend itself and share its uniquely evolved social mores.

4

The United States is now the world's most religiously diverse society (Eck, *A New Religious America*). We would be remiss to pursue our own religious practices as though they existed entirely independently from interaction with other communities and practitioners.

As manifested throughout Jewish history, our beliefs, ideas, and even self-understanding have been shaped through interaction with other traditions. From Alexander the Great's conquest of the Middle East and the Hellenistic influence on Rabbinic thought to al-Andalus

(Muslim-controlled Spain) in which we re-imbibed elements of Greek philosophical thought, and from French culture in the words and phrases that dot Rashi's commentaries to the Pale of Settlement and the kind of clothing that still demarcates Chasidim, it is evident that Judaism has seldom existed in isolation, in any of its forms.

The principle that has, however, transcended time, place, and external influence has been the need to pursue justice both within and beyond the bounds of the Jewish community. For us, as Jews living in the diverse American society, we can most effectively pursue a just society through engagement and partnership with other religious individuals and communities. Dialogue must exist as a precondition for action (or, at times, action as a precondition for deeper, more open dialogue). Shared interests and the universal need for a fair and good society extend beyond the bounds of any religious community. Trust and goodwill between communities intrinsically strengthens our society.

RABBI RACHEL TIMONER

1

Liberal Jews in our era treasure our autonomy and are ambivalent about the authority of God and Torah. No one is going to tell us what to say, what to do, or what to believe. Though we want the benefits of community, we are wary of the demands it may place on us. Furthermore, those of us in America live in a society in which freedom is defined in direct contrast to obligation, instead of in partnership with it.

But let's face it: we have not yet learned how to be free. It is one thing to throw off authority. It is another to realize freedom. Freedom requires conscious choice, and choice is its own burden. How do we choose well? Using which values? Having chosen, do we commit and follow through? How and when do we reevaluate our choices? The number and scope of choices in a day is overwhelming. Without a framework, we flail. So we look to a mix of external norms and institutions from the surrounding culture—the Protestant work ethic, the American dream, parenting trends, to name a few examples—to make choices for us. Shouldn't the wisdom of our own people have at least as strong a voice? Once we realize that we've traded one system of external authority for others, we find that the treasure we are seeking is under our own hearth. We are yearning for guidance. We are yearning for coherence. If chosen, covenant, mitzvah, and Torah are as relevant and sacred to us now as they ever have been.

Covenant is the choice to commit to a Jewish way of life in relationship with Jewish community: to study it, question it, and reinterpret it, but to choose Jewish text and tradition—the three-thousand-year-old conversation of our people with God—as a framework for our lives. Within this framework, a mitzvah is a call for action that requires a carefully considered response. Perhaps the response is to try to live the mitzvah for a period of time. Perhaps the response is commitment to the mitzvah, or rejection of it, or a "not yet." New mitzvot might be identified and adopted, old mitzvot might be reinterpreted or adapted. Decisions are made with care, lived out, and reevaluated in time. In this way, mitzvot become living expressions of our Jewish values, a thoughtful effort to learn the discipline of acting on our highest ideals. Through it all, Torah is our sacred guide. Those who study it know that it endlessly reveals insights about the meaning of life. Gershom Scholem teaches, "The Torah turns a special face to every single Jew, meant only for him [*sic*] and apprehensible only by him, and a Jew therefore fulfills his true purpose only when he comes to see this face and is able to incorporate it into the tradition" (Scholem, "Revelation and Tradition as Religious Categories in Judaism," 295).

Autonomy is a lonely fiction. Covenant, mitzvah, and Torah are the modern liberal Jew's way to journey toward freedom.

2

I put
יהוה
before me always. (Psalm 16:8)

You are not the center of the universe.
Remembering that is the beginning
of being religious.

What is the center of the universe?
That is the question of being religious.

Putting that question
and what's found there—
the Ineffable,
יהוה
—

before you always,
deliberately, repeatedly,
that is being religious.

You lift up the fallen . . . and are faithful to those who sleep in the dust.
(Birkat G'vurah, Amidah)

Having faith is different.
Having faith (*emunah*, אֱמוּנָה) is trusting that
when everything comes apart
and you fall,
you will be caught.

From generation to generation we will tell of your greatness.
(*K'dushah*)

If you're a religious Jew you testify
through words (*t'filot*) and actions (mitzvot)
to what you found
when you went asking
about the center of the universe.
You do so in chorus with your people,
singing through time.

You do so to remind yourself
that you are not at the center,
and What Is.

3

Any way you look at it, the Jewish people has a unique vocation among all nations. This does not make us superior. It only makes us singular. (The same can be said of every other tribe and nation on earth.) No other people shares our ancestry, our history, our Torah, our culture, our traditions, or our obligation.

You do not have to believe in God or Torah to believe in the unique vocation of the Jews. You only have to believe in history. Whether because, as the Torah teaches, God lifted us out of slavery in order to form an eternal covenant with our people; or because we witnessed, perished in, and survived the Holocaust; or because of a myriad of other defining moments in our story, the Jewish people is unlike any other. And we have a specific job to do.

We are here to remind the human race that the world we live in is not good enough, that human dignity, justice, and peace are possible on earth, and that we are needed to transform the world that is into the world that should be. As Tal Becker of the Shalom Hartman Institute wrote, "The Biblical imperative of being 'a kingdom of priests and a holy people' (Exodus 19:6) compels you not only to ask how can I be better tomorrow than I was today, but also to believe that constant improvement is possible" (Becker, "iEngage: How to Be an Optimist in the Middle East").

The prophets describe a messianic age when there will be dignity for the poor and justice for the oppressed (Isaiah 11:4), an end to all war among nations (Isaiah 2:4), harmony with nature (Isaiah 4:2), and an utter lack of fear (Micah 4:4).

I believe that human beings are capable of continual improvement and that the messianic age will be its result. If that day is guaranteed through God's will, we are needed as God's partners to make it real. If that day is not guaranteed by God, well then, it depends on us. Either way, I agree with Franz Kafka, who wrote: "The Messiah will come only when he is no longer necessary" (*Parables and Paradoxes, 81*).

4

On that day, God will be One and God's name will be One.

–*Aleinu* (based on Zechariah 14:9)

If our vision is to coexist in harmony with the other nations of the earth, if we dream that someday all will see that the many gods known to humanity are diverse faces of One and the same, we have a lot of work to do.

It begins with knowing each other. Organized dialogue in which churches and synagogues compare and contrast beliefs and values is important, but so are college friendships, neighbors walking the dogs together, sports teams, and book groups. What we need are real relationships of trust that enable Jews to know non-Jews, and non-Jews to know Jews, to ask each other honest questions over a cup of coffee or at the water cooler. We need safe friends with whom we can clear up misunderstandings, share perspectives, learn, and teach.

But in order to effectively field the questions of our non-Jewish friends and neighbors, to be able to explain the nature and origin of our holidays, theology, mitzvot, and customs, we have a lot of learning to do. To explain synagogue practice and life-cycle events, the role of Torah in our lives, the range of movements in contemporary Judaism, and our relationship with Israel, we first need to become Jewishly literate ourselves.

The Jewish people are not merely a faith community. We are a nation, a people, a collection of tribes. Exchange with adherents of other religious traditions is important, but equally important is dialogue with other ethnic, social, and cultural groups within the societies in which we live.

The most important question is not whether Jews are obligated to participate in intergroup dialogue. The most important question is, given the ubiquitous interaction between Jews and non-Jews: What is the nature of the dialogue already taking place? How effectively are Jews able to represent our own story and practice? What are non-Jews learning about Judaism from their Jewish friends, and what should they be learning? What should Jews be learning from non-Jews that will better equip us to understand and respect the other?

There are two goals here: (1) to educate ourselves to be able to represent Judaism and the Jewish people, and (2) to build greater trust and understanding between Jews and non-Jews so that we can create a future of peace and mutual respect.

RABBI MARY L. ZAMORE

1

I am not chosen; I choose.

A fourth-generation Reform Jew, I grew up in an active, religious household. By the time my bat mitzvah preparations came around, after an enthusiastic and very early start, I had grown into a kid who did not care for Hebrew school. Yet, I continued through confirmation because it was the default path in my family. Despite my apathy for religious school, I completely enjoyed the communal family observances of celebrating holidays and even attending services. I did not see myself as being actively part of Judaism. I went along for the ride, clinging to my parents and much older brother's coattails as they enthusiastically embraced their religion. Yet, when I was about seventeen years old sitting at my family seder, I was swept into a passionate discussion about some aspect of the Haggadah. I found myself thinking, "I like this. I really like this. I like Judaism for myself, not as an extension of my family." In that moment, I chose Judaism. Ever since then, I continue to choose Judaism.

I bind myself to the *b'rit* (בְּרִית), the covenant of Judaism, because I choose to accept the gift bequeathed to me by my family. Judaism has chosen me through my DNA and through my upbringing. Yet, nature and nurture did not stick until I actively accepted the gift. I now know Judaism is a beautiful, complex, complicated legacy. My task is to embrace, preserve, and help Judaism evolve.

Through educated choice, I have the ability to pick and choose the mitzvot to which I adhere. Because I bind myself to the law and do not believe that God will punish me for failing to uphold the mitzvot, I must be judicious in exercising my privilege to pick and choose, for it is tempting to select based on whim and convenience or, worse, hubris. Instead, I must remember that I will never understand the totality of our history, texts, and insights. That takes an entire generation to do, if it is possible at all. I can only absorb, synthesize, nurture, and finally pass on those parts of Judaism to which I attach, fit, and complement naturally. As I decide how to construct my Jewish life, I must weigh the collective wisdom of our tradition against my imperfect knowledge and experience. Furthermore, I am informed by two understandings: (1) the Torah—meaning the Five Books, the greater Hebrew Bible, and all of halachah (הֲלָכָה), "Jewish law," as developed over the ages, including the liberal contributions to the canon—has been shaped and forged by 3,500 years of generations of Jews; (2) I meet and hear God through our sacred texts yet am unsure of God's exact role in their formation.

When I make choices as to which mitzvot I uphold and which I disregard and which I take on as is and which I innovate, I remember my role in the ongoing transmission of the tradition. I value this legacy and strive to be a worthy guarantor of our tradition and its ongoing development.

2

I am religious and have faith.

Having faith does not mean that I believe that God micromanages my life, my fate, or human history. I do not expect God to fix my problems, save my loved ones from harm, or end war (although I frequently pray requesting those outcomes). God has created humanity with the capacity for compassion and good. When we focus our wisdom, talent, and empathy toward helping one another, we can accomplish much.

When our energies go toward callousness, destruction, and evil, we can destroy much. I have faith that God has created us in a manner that will favor our capacity for the constructive over the destructive. I have faith that when personal or communal challenges arise, we each have the innate ability to face those struggles, seek help, and receive the support, help, and empathy we will need to overcome or endure the challenges the randomness of life has wrought. Having faith means believing in what I cannot see or touch; it means believing in hope even when it seems distant.

Engaged religious practice, just like deep faith, has little to do with the type of expression of Judaism one chooses. Being religious means I see life through my Judaism, and my active engagement with Judaism is formed around prayer, study, and acts of social action and justice. I hope prayer and study, while useful activities in and of themselves, will strengthen my resolve to act with kindness in the world and fix that which is within my grasp. While I do not expect God to answer my prayers directly, I know personal prayer is a useful support for daily living, especially during stressful times, and communal prayer is a powerful practice that connects the individual to the generations and to the present community. Prayer lifts the spirit, calms anxiety, and gives voice to our deepest feelings—joy, despair, and the tedium that lives between the other two peaks. Gathering in a prayer community magnifies the human experience, raises our prayers in song, poetry, and narrative, and gives us perspective as we share our journeys with one another.

3

I believe in a different messianic age.

I believe in *y'mot hamashiach*, the messianic age, not in the traditional sense, but rather meaning the deepest desire and belief that we imperfect human beings can do better. In some ways, this is a supreme act of faith. As I witness the violence humans inflict on one another and on our earth, I waver in my faith in humanity's capacity to redeem itself. Yet, despite my temporary despair, I believe that we have the will and ability to put an end to violence and war, hunger and homelessness, hatred and bigotry, pollution and global warming.

I wish I could believe that God will bring an end of days and reward the good mitzvah doers with the perfect world-to-come, but I do not. My age of perfection is going to take a lot of hard work, most of which has defined ends and undefined paths. For example, peace is a clear goal, but the way there is complicated. Yet, God has given us the innate tools to make it happen, but we need to figure it out. Moving toward a better world will take a lot of hard work, but humanity will finally grow weary of the status quo and realize that our energy and money can create a more peaceful, equitable, and sustainable world.

Be warned: there will be no total perfection. Again, I wish there could be, but I do not believe it will be so. There will always be illness, accidents, and probably some violence. There will always be movement toward better, but we will never obtain perfection.

4

Interfaith dialogue is important.

Generations ago when the Jews came to America, the societal goal was to conform into the white, Anglo-Saxon, Protestant melting pot. Even when one retained a different ethnic background or religion or had a different skin color or body type, Protestant identity, affinity, and behavior was the model of success. The cultural revolution of the 1960s and 1970s brought a new celebration and pride in ethnic, racial, and religious identity. Sociologists talked about the tapestry of American society in which many identities came together under one flag. Today, there is a societal wave toward a new melting pot, not with an idealized white, Anglo-Saxon, Protestant identity as its goal, but rather a pareve, secular American identity loosely hung on commercialized Christianity. The underlying script says that we can all peacefully live together if we abandon separate identities in order to embrace common holidays, most of which are celebrated at the mall.

Judaism and Jewish identity are important, but not more important than other people's identities, beliefs, and religions. It is my identity, my religion—therefore it is unique, special, and holy to me. Being a Jew does not mean that I am better than others or closer to God; it just means that I have embraced the 3,500-year-old legacy bequeathed to me. I am its custodian, carefully accepting it and then transmitting it to the next generation.

Interfaith dialogue allows us to celebrate and appreciate each other's faith traditions. Time spent together dispels stereotypes and misinformation. Pain, hurt, and even hatred can be expressed and, hopefully, understood, perhaps even dispelled. New ways of relating can be formed; bridges can be built.

For Jews, interfaith dialogue is not only an important means to understand others, but also a vital mode to combat anti-Semitism and anti-Zionism. When we openly share our feelings and pain over world opinion of Jews and Israel, we educate others. Of course, we need to open our hearts equally to other faiths and their truths.

At its best, interfaith dialogue is a vehicle toward peace, bringing us closer to a better world.

Afterword

Ninety-five years ago, Hebrew Union College president Dr. Kaufmann Kohler published his magnum opus *Jewish Theology Systematically and Historically Considered.* His work bore an authoritative tone that rested on his prodigious scholarship and on his confidence in the strength of rational argument. Following Dr. Kohler by fifty years, Jewish theologian and Hebrew Union College professor Eugene Borowitz wrote:

> For just as history no longer shows a single progressive march of Jewish faith, so contemporary philosophy does not provide a single standard of truth so widely accepted that it might become the foundation of a theology of Judaism. . . .
>
> Perhaps, then, one should only do theology rather than try to write a theology. That would mean working on individual themes without being too much concerned about what interconnects them. (Borowitz, *New Jewish Theology*, 218–19)

The work and views of Drs. Kohler and Borowitz may not be as mutually distancing as one might think. Kohler clearly kept the door open to ongoing theological inquiry and creative exploration:

> For in my opinion, the Jewish religion has never been static, fixed for all time by an ecclesiastical authority, but has ever been the result of a dynamic process of growth and development. . . . Revelation is to be considered as a continuous force shaping and re-shaping the Jewish faith. (Kohler, *Jewish Theology*, xliv–xlv)

Dr. Borowitz has inspired countless students and readers throughout his professional life with his lucid expression and advocacy of covenant theology. He personally has been one who not only "does theology," but one who writes about theology with reasoned intention and persuasiveness. In numerous ways, he has met his stated goal:

> Jewish theology is the effort to set forth this hopeful faith in self-conscious, intellectual form." (Borowitz, *New Jewish Theology*, 43)

Lights in the Forest is a book that represents something of both Kohler's and Borowitz's views. This anthology is not a systematic theological presentation, nor is it definitive in its scope and ideas. It has compiled the thoughts of rabbis who "do theology" as a result of answering the questions of fellow Jews and students. The faith they express bears out Dr. Kohler's notion of the "dynamic process" in Judaism's growth and development.

The responses of the thirty-nine rabbis within this volume are bound together by a vibrant and essential connective tissue: all seek meaning and the affirmation of values in the soil of Judaism. This commitment holds together the spectrum of their teachings. Further, it seems that each of the contributors draws his or her position from three sources: critical thinking, personal experience, and study.

Critical thinking has led our contributors to reject the traditional biblical image of an anthropomorphic, male, ruling God. Their critical thinking has also, perhaps paradoxically, brought them to vivid awareness that there are valid horizons of knowing beside and beyond reason alone. Our writers acknowledge that their views have been in flux for a lifetime, and they expect such evolution to continue.

Personal experience is for many a cornerstone of building theological views. Among our contributors are children of Holocaust survivors, alumni of the Religious Action Center (the social justice arm of Reform Judaism), graduates of Reform Jewish summer camps and youth group programs, a Jew-by-choice, those from more traditional backgrounds and those from more secular backgrounds, a graduate of Hebrew Union College–Jewish Institute of Religion's Israeli rabbinic program, and an eyewitness to mass death in Darfur. Some rabbis draw on their experience of personal family celebration, on the spiritual environment of the High Holy Days, or from the privilege of conducting life-cycle ceremonies. Personal experience has heightened, in their thinking and in their lives, compassion, humaneness, and receptivity to God's ubiquitous presence.

Rabbis question and doubt, just as all Jews do. Rabbinic education exposes them to a variety of teachers and expressions, which ultimately shape their own thinking. When we read the personal ideas of contemporary rabbis in *Lights in the Forest*, we hear through them biblical voices and the voices of the ancient sages. We hear Maimonides and Rashi. The teachings of Kaplan, Heschel, Buber, and Baeck speak through them. Modern Hebrew literature, the thought of physicists, and the writings of David Ellenson, Eugene Borowitz, Lawrence Kushner, David Hartman, Judith Plaskow, and Harold Kushner are apparent and present.

Few of us develop ideas that are not influenced by others. Likewise, the context of our social, political, historical, and philosophical framework shapes the direction and core of our views. Bearing in mind such contemporary influence and frames, we have found some key ongoing themes in this anthology:

- We must be receptive by both rational and non-rational means, through experience and mindfulness, to God's eternal presence.
- Our essence as humans is related to the Divine. All existing elements of Creation are one, part of the Divine.
- *B'rit* (בְּרִית), "covenant," asks us to commit ourselves voluntarily to human freedom and to the ideals and deeds of creating a just society. *B'rit* is a communal endeavor, not merely a personal or individual one. We need to be an inclusive community of all Jews who wish to affirm a commitment to *b'rit.*
- Jewish ritual makes us more aware, compassionate, and connected as Jewish human beings.
- Being religious means participating in ongoing Jewish activities: prayer, study, communal involvement, and social justice.

One might well ask: if the Reform Movement is a pluralistic expression of Judaism, how is it possible that the five core themes we have noted tend to be shared by our thirty-nine rabbinic respondents? Rabbis today face and respond to some very pressing questions. How does the modern liberal Jew balance personal autonomy and freedom with a sense of responsibility and obligation? How can we remain critical thinkers in the realm of belief and also be open to experience and intuition? How do we apportion our loyalty and devotion to the Jewish people while still finding ways to serve humanity? The rabbis here who ponder these questions in the context of our times do provide some overlapping views. The richness of their answers and their ability to speak to individual readers rest in their diversity of expression and in the nuances of their focus. In the end, their responses reflect a liberal questioning and critical approach to Jewish traditional texts. They are comfortable using metaphor as a means of teaching. They demonstrate openness to considering both secular and non-Western ways of thinking. All are eager to convey their insights to the broad Jewish community.

All of the rabbis who answered our questions did so with enthusiasm and caring about this project. Their passion is to learn and to teach, to listen and to understand. We are of one mind and intention, namely, to deepen the love and value Jews have for Judaism. We wish, through this volume, to encourage further study and ongoing questioning, for we know that a fulfilling Jewish existence cannot be based solely on recalling the Holocaust or worrying about intermarriage. Jewish life, practice, and identity make sense only when Jews perceive Judaism's intellectual and spiritual tools as the means for fashioning an exalted life of purpose and commitment. With such a goal before us, we keep in mind as a touchstone these words of hope:

> You shall seek Me and find Me, when you search for Me with all your heart. (Jeremiah 29:13)

Contributors

Rabbi Lee Bycel is the spiritual leader of Congregation Beth Shalom in Napa, California. He is also an adjunct professor of Jewish Studies and Social Justice at the University of San Francisco as well as a senior moderator at the Aspen Institute. For over fifteen years, he served as dean of the Hebrew Union College-Jewish Institute of Religion, Los Angeles, including as director of the rabbinic school. Since 2004 he has made several humanitarian trips to Darfur refugee camps and has raised major funding for medical and emergency aid for the refugee community.

Rabbi Kenneth Chasen is senior rabbi of Leo Baeck Temple in Los Angeles and an outspoken commentator and author on a wide variety of subjects pertaining to Jewish life, with a special emphasis on social justice in the United States and in Israel. His writings have appeared in a wide variety of books and national and international publications, including the *Los Angeles Times*, *New York Times*, *Chicago Tribune*, *Reform Judaism*, and *Jewish Journal*, among many others. Rabbi Chasen is also the co-author of two books that guide Jewish families in the creation of meaningful Jewish rituals in the home. In addition, he is a nationally recognized composer whose original liturgical and educational works are regularly heard in synagogues, religious schools, Jewish camps, and sanctuaries across North America and in Israel.

Rabbi Micah Citrin grew up at Congregation Albert in Albuquerque, New Mexico. After serving as an associate rabbi at Congregation Beth

Am in Los Altos Hills, California, and Peninsula Temple Beth El in San Mateo, California, he is currently co-senior rabbi with his wife, Rabbi Karen Citrin, at Temple Israel in Tulsa, Oklahoma. Rabbi Citrin has a degree in history from the University of Oregon and attended rabbinical school at Hebrew Union College–Jewish Institute of Religion in Los Angeles, where he also received a master's degree in Jewish education. He was ordained in 2005. Rabbi Micah is a father of twin boys. When Rabbi Micah is not at Temple Israel, he can be found running along the banks of the Arkansas River.

Rabbi Mike Comins directs the Making Prayer Real Course (MakingPrayerReal.com) and the TorahTrek Center for Jewish Wilderness Spirituality (TorahTrek.org), including the TorahTrek Guides Track, a yearlong, three-retreat training program for Jewish leaders. He is author of *Making Prayer Real: Leading Jewish Spiritual Voices on Why Prayer Is Difficult and What to Do about It* and *A Wild Faith: Jewish Ways into Wilderness, Wilderness Ways into Judaism*. A yeshiva-trained, Israeli-ordained Reform rabbi and a licensed Israeli desert guide, Rabbi Comins holds an MA in Jewish education (Hebrew University) with an emphasis in contemporary philosophy. He received extensive training in meditation, Hebrew chant, qigong, and spiritual practice in the natural world.

Rabbi Benjamin David is the senior rabbi of Adath Emanu-El in Mount Laurel, New Jersey. He is the co-founder of Running Rabbis, a nonprofit initiative that promotes creative forms of social action. He and his wife, Lisa, have three children.

Rabbi Geoffrey W. Dennis (Hebrew Union College–Jewish Institute of Religion, Cincinnati, 1996) is rabbi of Congregation Kol Ami in Flower Mound, Texas, as well as an adjunct professor in the Jewish Studies Program of the University of North Texas. He is the author of one book, *The Encyclopedia of Jewish Myth, Magic, and Mysticism*, and of numerous academic and professional articles. His most recent, "Your Kisses Are Sweeter than Wine: Jewish Erotic Theology," appears in *Sacred Encounters* (CCAR Press, 2013).

Rabbi Denise L. Eger is the founding rabbi of Congregation Kol Ami in West Hollywood, California. She has been a rabbi in the Los Angeles area for more than twenty-five years and will be President of the Central Conference of American Rabbis (CCAR) for the 2015–2017 term. She writes extensively on Judaism and human sexuality and continues to be an advocate and activist for LGBT equality.

Rabbi Dena A. Feingold (Hebrew Union College–Jewish Institute of Religion, Cincinnati, 1982) has served Beth Hillel Temple in Kenosha, Wisconsin, since 1985. She became Wisconsin's first female rabbi when named assistant rabbi at Congregation Shalom in Milwaukee in 1982. Rabbi Feingold has been an active participant in interfaith work and social justice causes throughout her career. She is married to Brad Backer and has two adult children, Jonathan and Abigail Backer.

Rabbi Michael S. Friedman has served as associate rabbi at Central Synagogue in New York City since 2008. Prior to this position, Michael was director of high school programs at the Union for Reform Judaism from 2004 to 2006 and assistant rabbi at Congregation B'nai Jeshurun in Short Hills, New Jersey, from 2006 to 2008. He holds a BA in history from Yale University and was ordained by Hebrew Union College–Jewish Institute of Religion in 2004. In his free time Michael likes to hike, play golf, run marathons, and cook.

Rabbi Stephen Lewis Fuchs is rabbi emeritus of Congregation Beth Israel, West Hartford, Connecticut. Upon his retirement from Beth Israel in 2011, he served as president of the World Union for Progressive Judaism, advocating for Reform Jewish ideals, practice, and legitimacy during visits to sixty-five communities on five continents. Before coming to Beth Israel in 1997, he served as the first full-time rabbi of Temple Isaiah, Columbia, Maryland, and as senior rabbi of Congregation Ohabai Sholom (the Temple) in Nashville, Tennessee. In the fall of 2013, he served as interim rabbi at Congregation Beth Shalom in Milan, Italy. He has been married to Victoria (Steinberg) since his ordination from Hebrew Union College–Jewish Institute of Religion in 1974 (blessed with three children and four grandchildren). He earned a doctor of ministry degree in biblical interpretation from Vanderbilt University Divinity School in 1992.

Rabbi George D. Gittleman has served as the spiritual leader of Congregation Shomrei Torah in Santa Rosa, California, since his ordination in 1996. He is also a Senior Rabbinic Fellow of the Shalom Hartman Institute in Jerusalem and a graduate of the Rabbinic Leadership Program of the Institute for Jewish Spirituality.

Rabbi Jeffrey W. Goldwasser is the spiritual leader of Temple Sinai, a Reform congregation in Cranston, Rhode Island. He was ordained by Hebrew Union College–Jewish Institute of Religion in New York City in 2000. Before serving Temple Sinai, he served congregations in Stuart, Florida and North Adams, Massachusetts. He is the author of the website *Reb Jeff*, a blog about living a joyful Jewish life and bringing joy to synagogues and the Jewish community.

Rabbi Oren J. Hayon was ordained from Hebrew Union College-Jewish Institute of Religion in 2004, and has dedicated his rabbinate to creating vibrant Jewish communities that provide engaging, meaningful content. His work focuses primarily on Jewish education and identity formation for young adults, and currently serves as the Greenstein Family Executive Director at the Hillel Foundation for Jewish Life at the University of Washington. He lives in Seattle with his wife and two daughters.

Rabbi Ammiel Hirsch is the senior rabbi of the Stephen Wise Free Synagogue in New York City, where he has led a dramatic revival of Jewish life. He is the former executive director of ARZA (Association of Reform Zionists of America) and was the chairman of the Central Conference of American Rabbis (CCAR) Tripartite Zionist Platform Committee (the Miami Platform). Rabbi Hirsch is the co-author of *One People, Two Worlds: A Reform Rabbi and an Orthodox Rabbi Explore the Issues That Divide Them*. Rabbi Hirsch received numerous awards for academic excellence from the Hebrew Union College–Jewish Institute of Religion and was ordained in 1989. He was admitted to the New York State Bar in 1984, after earning his LLB (honors) degree from the London School of Economics and Political Science, where he was a recipient of the Barclay Scholarship.

Rabbi Bruce Kadden has served as rabbi of Temple Beth El in Tacoma, Washington since July 2004. He received an AB degree in Religious Studies from Stanford University in 1976 and was ordained by Hebrew Union College-Jewish Institute of Religion in Cincinnati, Ohio in 1981. He previously served as assistant rabbi of Mount Zion Temple in St. Paul, Minnesota and as rabbi of Temple Beth El in Salinas, California. He is past president of the Pacific Association of Reform Rabbis. He and his wife, Barbara Binder Kadden, are the authors of *Teaching Mitzvot: Concepts, Values and Activities; Teaching Tefilah: Insights and Activities on Prayer;* and *Teaching Jewish Life Cycle: Traditions and Activities.*

Rabbi Yoel Kahn is the rabbi of Congregation Beth El, Berkeley, California. He was ordained by Hebrew Union College–Jewish Institute of Religion in 1985 and received his PhD from the Graduate Theological Union. His book *The Three Blessings: Boundaries, Censorship and Identity in Jewish Liturgy* was published in 2010. He writes and teaches about Jewish theology, liturgy, and spirituality.

Rabbi Paul Kipnes leads Congregation Or Ami, Calabasas, California, and is number 51 on *Newsweek*'s "Top 50 Rabbis" list. He teaches at Hebrew Union College–Jewish Institute of Religion. Under his leadership, Congregation Or Ami has won ten awards for social justice, innovative worship, interfaith outreach, and best synagogue use of technology. It wins hearts for reaching out during times of need. Rabbi Kipnes co-edited the issue of *CCAR Journal* on "New Visions for Jewish Community," serves Jews recovering from addictions, and blogs at rabbipaul.blogspot.com.

Rabbi Zoë Klein is the senior rabbi of Temple Isaiah in Los Angeles. She is the author of the novel *Drawing in the Dust*, which was published by Simon and Schuster in 2009, of which Publishers Weekly wrote, "Insight into the world of biblical excavation in Israel raises Rabbi Klein's debut novel from a Jewish *Da Vinci Code* to an emotionally rich story of personal and historical discovery."

Rabbi Sue Levi Elwell, PhD, edited *Chapters of the Heart: Jewish Women Sharing the Torah of Our Lives* (2013), *The Open Door Haggadah* (CCAR Press, 2002), and *Lesbian Rabbis: The First Generation* (2001); and served as poetry editor for *The Torah: A Women's Commentary* (URJ Press, 2008). She has served as a congregational rabbi, as the founding director of the Los Angeles Feminist Center, and as the first rabbinic director of Ma'yan: The Jewish Women's Project of the JCC of Manhattan. From 1996 to 2014 she worked with congregational leaders through the Union for Reform Judaism.

Rabbi Rachel S. Mikva, PhD, currently serves as the Schaalman Chair in Jewish Studies and director of the Center for Jewish, Christian, and Islamic Studies at Chicago Theological Seminary. Although Dr. Mikva's areas of deepest expertise are rabbinic literature and the history of scriptural interpretation, she teaches a range of Jewish and comparative studies, with a special interest in the intersections of Scripture, culture, and ethics.

Rabbi Evan Moffic serves as senior rabbi of Congregation Solel in Highland Park, Illinois. A graduate of Stanford University, he was ordained in 2006. He is the author of *Wisdom for People of All Faiths: Ten Ways to Connect with God* (2013). He also blogs for the *Huffington Post*, Beliefnet.com, and his personal website, Rabbi.me.

Rabbi Jay Henry Moses is the director of The Wexner Heritage Program, North America's premier adult Jewish learning and leadership program for outstanding volunteer Jewish communal leaders, at the Wexner Foundation. Previously, he was the associate rabbi at Temple Sholom of Chicago. His writing has appeared in two volumes of Lawrence A. Hoffman's *My People's Prayer Book* series and in numerous journals, magazines, and newspapers. He lives in Columbus, Ohio, with his wife, Cantor Bat-Ami Moses, and their two sons.

Rabbi Debra J. Robbins has served as a member of the clergy team at Temple Emanu-El in Dallas since her ordination from the Hebrew Union College-Jewish Institute of Religion in 1991. She has been fortunate to work in partnership with many lay leaders and professional staff members across the congregation and especially enjoys her work teaching adults. She has developed lasting programs and projects in many areas of the synagogue that have engaged members of all ages in deepening their connections to each other, to Jewish living, and to God. She contributes leadership to the Dallas community by serving as chair of the Vaad Hamikvah, has served nationally on the Executive Committee of the CCAR and as Convention Chair, and is president of Reading Village, an international organization working on issues of leadership and literacy in rural Guatemala. Rabbi Robbins continues to grow in her rabbinate, educationally and spiritually by her involvement with the Institute for Jewish Spirituality.

Rabbi Jason Rosenberg is the rabbi of Congregation Beth Am in Tampa, Florida. Rabbi Rosenberg was ordained by the Hebrew Union College—Jewish Institute of Religion in 2001, in New York. Before going to Tampa, Rabbi Rosenberg was the associate rabbi at Holy Blossom Temple in Toronto, Ontario, and before that he was a software engineer, having received a degree in computer science from Brown University. Still a scientist at heart, Rabbi Rosenberg believes in a Judaism which is devotedly rational and that uses the mind as well as the spirit, each strengthening the other.

Rabbi Judith Schindler has been senior rabbi of Temple Beth El in Charlotte, North Carolina, since 2003. Rabbi Schindler is past co-chair of the Women's Rabbinic Network and is active on many local and national boards. She has envisioned and led the creation of three award-winning documentaries that are being used across the country as tools for advocacy and education: "Souls of Our Students," on diversity and inclusion; "Souls of Our Teachers," on urban education; and "Souls of Our Neighbors," on affordable housing. In addition to receiving many humanitarian awards, she was named Charlotte Woman of the Year in 2011.

Rabbi Ariana Silverman graduated from Harvard University, is an alumna of the Wexner Graduate Fellowship Program, and after ordination, moved to Detroit, where she currently works with young Jewish adults. She served as the assistant rabbi at Temple Kol Ami in West Bloomfield, Michigan, and has worked for the Religious Action Center of Reform Judaism, the Coalition on the Environment and Jewish Life, the Sierra Club, Hazon, Temple Beth Israel in Steubenville, Ohio, and Congregation Emanu-El of the City of New York. She is believed to be the only rabbi living within Detroit's city limits and frequently can be found teaching about Judaism while working in a garden.

Rabbi Suzanne Singer is the rabbi and the educator at Temple Beth El in Riverside, California. Previously she served Temple Sinai in Oakland. She was ordained by Hebrew Union College–Jewish Institute of Religion in 2003, and was awarded prizes in Bible, Midrash, Liturgy, and ethics. Two of her essays were published in *The Torah: A Women's Commentary* (URJ Press). Prior to becoming a rabbi in 2003, she was a television producer and programming executive for national public television, for which she won two national Emmy awards.

Rabbi Joseph A. Skloot is completing his PhD in Jewish history at Columbia University, where he studies the history of Jewish culture in the early modern and modern periods. He writes about the connection between technological innovation and cultural change, particularly with regard to printing. He received rabbinic ordination from Hebrew Union College–Jewish Institute of Religion and an AB in history from Princeton. A recipient of numerous academic and community awards, including a Jacob K. Javits Graduate Fellowship and a Tisch Rabbinical Fellowship, he teaches Torah to students of all ages at synagogues across the country.

Rabbi Joshua Stanton serves as an assistant rabbi at Temple B'nai Jeshurun in Short Hills, New Jersey. During rabbinical school, Josh served as associate director of the Center for Global Judaism at Hebrew College and director of communications for the Coexist Foundation. He was also a founding co-editor of the *Journal of Inter-Religious Dialogue*, as well as *O.N. Scripture—The Torah*, a weekly online Torah commentary featured on the *Huffington Post*. Josh was one of six finalists worldwide for the 2012 Coexist Prize and was additionally highlighted by the Coexist Forum as "one of the foremost Jewish and interreligious bloggers in the world."

Rabbi Lance J. Sussman, PhD, began his service as the eighth senior rabbi of Reform Congregation Keneseth Israel in July 2001. Rabbi

Sussman has published numerous books and articles, including *Isaac Lesser and the Making of American Judaism* and *Sharing Sacred Moments* (a collection of his sermons), and has served as an editor of *Reform Judaism in America: A Biographical Dictionary and Sourcebook*. He has appeared in several PBS specials on Judaism in America and has co-produced a documentary of his own, *Voices for Justice* with Dr. Gary P. Zola. Rabbi Sussman served as national chair of the CCAR Press, the publishing arm of the Central Conference of American Rabbis, for ten years and recently was elected president of the Association for Progressive Judaism, an independent Reform think tank based in New York City. He is a trustee of the Katz Center for Advanced Judaic Studies at the University of Pennsylvania, the American Jewish Historical Society (NY), and is an active member of the Academic Advisory and Editorial Board of the American Jewish Archives (Cincinnati). Previously, Rabbi Sussman served as chair of the Jewish Studies Department at Binghamton University-SUNY and has offered courses in Jewish history at Hebrew Union College-Jewish Institute of Religion in New York City and Princeton University. He currently teaches American Jewish History at Princeton University and Modern Jewish History at Temple University and Gratz College.

Rabbi Rachel Timoner is the associate rabbi at Leo Baeck Temple, Los Angeles, where her work centers on community building, social justice, spiritual life, and lifelong learning. She grew up in Miami, Florida, received a BA from Yale University, and received *s'michah* from Hebrew Union College–Jewish Institute of Religion in 2009, where she was a Wexner Graduate Fellow and received numerous honors. Rabbi Timoner is the author of *Breath of Life: God as Spirit in Judaism*. She is married to Felicia Park-Rogers, and they have two sons, Benjamin and Eitan.

Rabbi Andrew Vogel is the rabbi of Temple Sinai in Brookline, Massachusetts, which he has served since 2004. He was ordained by the Hebrew Union College–Jewish Institute of Religion in New York in

1998 and has served Reform congregations in Marietta, Georgia, and Wayland, Massachusetts. He lives in Newton Centre with his wife, Martha Hausman, and their two daughters.

Rabbi Max Weiss serves as rabbi of Oak Park Temple, B'nai Abraham Zion, in Oak Park, Illinois. He has served on a variety of committees and boards including the Jewish United Fund of Chicago, Olin Sang Ruby Union Institute, where he volunteers every Summer; an ethics board at a local hospital; and various interfaith groups around Chicago. Rabbi Weiss is married and has three children.

Rabbi Stanton Zamek has been the spiritual leader of the United Jewish Congregation of Hong Kong since 2008. Prior to coming to the UJC, Rabbi Zamek served congregations in Baton Rouge, Louisiana, and San Francisco, California. Rabbi Zamek was ordained by the Hebrew Union College-Jewish Institute of Religion in 1996, in the same class as his wife, Rabbi Martha Bergadine, the UJC's director of Education and Programming. Rabbi Zamek and Rabbi Bergadine have two children. Prior to entering the seminary, Rabbi Zamek practiced law in Chicago, Illinois. He has a JD from Northwestern University School of Law.

Rabbi Mary L. Zamore was ordained by Hebrew Union College-Jewish Institute of Religion in New York in 1997 and serves the Jewish Center of Northwest Jersey in Washington, New Jersey. An active writer and editor, she is best known for *The Sacred Table: Creating a Jewish Food Ethic* (CCAR Press, 2011), which was designated a finalist by the National Jewish Book Awards.

Rabbi Elaine Zecher has served as a member of the clergy of Temple Israel, Boston, since 1990. Her rabbinate has focused on ways to nurture one's inner life. She has developed and implemented many programs and opportunities touching the lives of Temple Israel's congregants from the very youngest to its most senior members in many significant and meaningful ways. Rabbi Zecher's work extends beyond the congregation. She sits on the New England Regional Board of the Anti-Defamation League, is Vice President for Leadership of the Central Conference of American Rabbis (CCAR), and serves as Chair of the *Machzor* Advisory Group for the CCAR. Rabbi Zecher served as chair of the Worship and Practices Committee of the CCAR and was actively involved in producing and editing *Mishkan T'filah: A Reform Siddur*. She received ordination from Hebrew Union College-Jewish Institute of Religion in 1988.

Rabbi Ben Zeidman is the assistant rabbi at Congregation Emanu-El of the City of New York. He was ordained by the Hebrew Union College-Jewish Institute of Religion in Cincinnati in 2010. He served as the Developmental Editor of *The New Union Haggadah, Revised Edition*, which was recently published. He lives on New York City's Upper East Side with his wife Katie, and his son Oliver.

Rabbi Or Zohar was born in Jerusalem, Israel. He lives in the Galilee with his family. He is the rabbi of Maalot Tivon Reform Congregation and is a former founding rabbi of Kehilat Halev in Tel Aviv. Rabbi Zohar is a teacher of Judaism and Kabbalah, a musician, and a radio broadcaster.

Rabbi Josh "Yoshi" Zweiback serves as head of school of Wise School in Los Angeles, California. He grew up in Omaha, Nebraska, studied religion at Princeton University, and received an MA in Jewish Education and then rabbinical ordination from Hebrew Union College-Jewish Institute of Religion. He is a senior rabbinic fellow of the Shalom Hartman Institute where he continues his learning in Jerusalem each summer. He records and performs music as part of Mah Tovu and is the founder and volunteer executive director of the Kavod Tzedakah Collective. He and his spouse, Jacqueline, have three daughters.

Works Consulted

Ablom, Mitch. *Tuesdays With Morrie*. New York: Broadway Books, 2002.

Adler, Rachel. *Engendering Judaism: An Inclusive Theology and Ethics*. Boston: Beacon Press, 1999.

Alter, Robert. *The Five Books of Moses: A Translation with Commentary*. New York: W.W. Norton, 2004.

Amichai, Yehudah. "HaZeman." In *Yehudah Amichai: A Life of Poetry, 1948–1994*, translated by Benjamin and Barbara Harshav, 275–76. New York: HarperCollins, 1995.

Baeck, Leo. *Judaism and Christianity: Essays*. Philadelphia: Jewish Publication Society, 1958.

Becker, Tal. "iEngage: How to Be an Optimist in the Middle East." *Jerusalem Post*, May 30, 2013. http://www.jpost.com/Opinion/Columnists/iEngage-How-to-be-an-optimist-in-the-Middle-East-314947.

Beker, Avi. *The Chosen: The History of an Idea, and the Anatomy of an Obsession*. New York: Palgrave Macmillan, 2008.

Berdichevsky, Micha Yosef. *Meditations*. 1899.

Borowitz, Eugene. *Choices in Modern Jewish Thought: A Partisan's Guide*. Springfield, NJ: Behrman House, 1995.

———. *A New Jewish Theology in the Making*. Philadelphia: Westminster Press, 1968.

———. *Renewing the Covenant*. Philadelphia: Jewish Publication Society, 1991.

Buber, Martin. *I and Thou*. New York: Charles Scribner & Sons, 1970.

———. *On Judaism*. New York: Schocken Books, 1967.

———. *Way of Man*. New York: Citadel Press, 1994.

Central Conference of American Rabbis (CCAR). Miami Platform, 1997. http://ccarnet.org/rabbis-speak/platforms/reform-judaism-zionism-centenary-platform/.

———. Pittsburgh Platform, 1885. http://ccarnet.org/rabbis-speak/platforms/declaration-principles/.

———. A Statement of Principles for Reform Judaism, 1999, http://ccarnet.org/platforms/principles.html. http://ccarnet.org/rabbis-speak/platforms/statement-principles-reform-judaism/.

Culi, Yaakov. *The Torah Anthology: Me'am Lo'ez.* Translated by Aryeh Kaplan. Vol. 1. New York: Moznaim, 1977.

Daley, Tad. "Earth to Mars: Choosing a Flag to Unite a Planet." *New York Times,* January 29, 2004.

Deutsch, David. *The Beginning of Infinity.* New York: Penguin Books, 2012.

Eck, Diana L. *A New Religious America: How a "Christian Country" Has Become the World's Most Religiously Diverse Nation.* San Francisco: HarperSanFrancisco, 2002.

Eskenazi, Tamara Cohn, and Andrea L. Weiss, eds. *The Torah: A Women's Commentary.* New York: URJ Press, 2008.

Ellenson, David. "Reform Zionism Today: A Consideration of First Principles." *Journal of Reform Zionism* 2 (1995):13–18.

Falk, Marcia. *The Book of Blessings.* San Francisco: HarperSanFrancisco, 1996.

Frishman, Elyse D., ed. *Mishkan T'filah: A Reform Siddur.* New York: CCAR, 2007.

Gillman, Neil. *The Death of Death: Resurrection and Immortality in Jewish Thought.* Woodstock, VT: Jewish Lights Publishing, 1997.

Gordon, Noah. *The Rabbi.* New York: McGraw-Hill, 1965. Open Road Media, 2012 e-book.

Green, Arthur. *Radical Judaism: Rethinking God and Tradition.* New Haven, CT: Yale University Press, 2010.

Greenberg, Irving. "Cloud of Smoke, Pillar of Fire: Judaism, Christianity, and Modernity after the Holocaust" (1974). In *Auschwitz: Beginning of a New Era?,* edited by Eva Fleischner. New York: Ktav Publishing House, 1977.

Hartman, David. *The God Who Hates Lies: Confronting & Rethinking Jewish Tradition.* Woodstock, VT: Jewish Lights Publishing, 2011.

———. *A Heart of Many Rooms: Celebrating the Many Voices within Judaism.* Woodstock, VT: Jewish Lights Publishing, 1999.

———. *The Living Covenant.* Woodstock, VT: Jewish Lights Publishing, 2003.

Heschel, Abraham Joshua. *God in Search of Man.* New York: Farrar, Straus and Giroux, 1955.

———. *Man Is Not Alone: A Philosophy of Religion.* New York: Farrar, Straus and Giroux, 1951.

———. *The Sabbath: Its Meaning for Modern Man.* New York: Farrar, Straus and Young, 1951.

———. *Who Is Man?* Stanford, CA: Stanford University Press, 1965.

Hirsch, Richard G. *From the Hill to the Mount: A Reform Zionist Quest.* New York: Gefen Publishing House, 2000.

Kafka, Franz. *Parables and Paradoxes.* New York: Schocken Books, 1961.

Kalmanofsky, Jeremy. "Cosmic Theology and Earthly Religion." In *Jewish Theology in Our Time*, edited by Elliot Cosgrove. Woodstock, VT: Jewish Lights Publishing, 2012.

Kaplan, Mordecai M. *Judaism as a Civilization: Toward a Reconstruction of American-Jewish Life.* Philadelphia: Jewish Publication Society, 2010.

———. "What Is Our Human Destiny?" *Judaism* 2, no. 3 (July 1953).

Kohler, Kaufmann. *Jewish Theology Systematically and Historically Considered.* New York: Ktav, 1968 (first published 1918).

Kukla, Eliot. "Terms for Gender Diversity in Classical Jewish Texts." TransTorah, 2006. http://transtorah.org/PDFs/Classical_Jewish_Terms_for_Gender_Diversity.pdf.

Kushner, Harold S. *To Life! A Celebration of Jewish Being and Thinking.* New York: Warner Books, 1993.

———. *When Bad Things Happen to Good People.* 20th anniversary ed. New York: Schocken Books, 2001.

Kushner, Lawrence. *Honey from the Rock: An Introduction to Jewish Mysticism.* Woodstock, VT: Jewish Lights Publishing, 2000.

———. *Invisible Lines of Connection.* Woodstock, VT: Jewish Lights, 1996.

Lamott, Anne. *Help, Thanks, Wow.* New York: Riverhead Books, 2012.

Levinas, Emmanuel. *Nine Talmudic Readings.* Bloomington: Indiana University Press, 1990.

"Marcion: Gospel of the Lord and Other Writings." Gnostic Society Library. http://www.gnosis.org/library/marcionsection.htm.

Matt, Daniel. *The Essential Kabbalah: The Heart of Jewish Mysticism.* San Francisco: HarperSanFrancisco, 1995.

———. *God and the Big Bang: Discovering Harmony between Science and Spirituality.* Woodstock, VT: Jewish Lights Publishing, 1998.

Michaelson, Jay. "Does Mysticism Prove the Existence of God?" *Zeek*, July 2005. http://www.zeek.net/jay_0507.shtml.

———. *Everything Is God: The Radical Path of Nondual Judaism.* Boston: Trumpeter, 2009.

———. *God vs. Gay? The Religious Case for Equality.* Boston: Beacon Press, 2011.

Opler, Edward Morris. *Myths and Tales of the Jicarilla Apache Indians.* New York: Dover Publications, 1994.

Pappenheim, Bertha. "The Jewish Woman in Religious Life." Translated by Margery Bentwich. In *Four Centuries of Jewish Women's Spirituality: A Sourcebook,* rev. ed., edited by Ellen M. Umansky and Dianne Ashton, Lebanon, NH: Brandeis University Press, 2009.

Petuchowski, Jakob Josef. *Guide to the Prayerbook.* Cincinnati: Hebrew Union College–Jewish Institute of Religion, 1992.

Plaskow, Judith. *Standing Again at Sinai: Judaism from a Feminist Perspective.* San Francisco: HarperSanFrancisco, 1991.

Plaut, W. Gunther, ed. *The Torah: A Modern Commentary.* Rev. ed. New York: URJ Press, 2005.

Pogrebin, Abigail. *Stars of David: Prominent Jews Talk about Being Jewish.* New York: Broadway Books, 2007.

Polish, David, ed. *Rabbi's Manual.* New York: CCAR, 1988.

Rabinowicz, Rachel Anne. *Passover Haggadah: The Feast of Freedom.* New York: United Synagogue Book Service, 1982.

Sacks, Jonathan. *To Heal a Fractured World.* New York: Schocken Books, 2005.

Schlipp, Paul Arthur, and Maurice S. Friedman, eds. *The Philosophy of Martin Buber.* London: Cambridge University Press, 1967.

Scholem, Gershom. "Revelation and Tradition as Religious Categories in Judaism." In *The Messianic Idea in Judaism.* New York: Schocken Books, 1971.

Schwarzschild, Steven. *In Pursuit of the Ideal: The Jewish Writing of Steven Schwarzschild.* Edited by Menachem Kellner. Albany, NY: SUNY Press, 1990.

Scult, Mel. *The Radical American Judiasm of Mordecai Kaplan.* Bloomington, IN: Indiana University Press, 2013.

Siegel, Danny. *And God Braided Eve's Hair.* New York: United Synagogue of America, 1980.

Silberstein, Laurence J., and Robert L. Cohn, eds. *The Other in Jewish Thought and History: Constructions of Jewish Culture and Identity.* New York: NYU Press, 1994.

Stanton, Joshua. "God as Ordering Force in the Universe," *Huffington Post,* September 9, 2012.

Stern, Chaim, ed. *Gates of Repentance: The New Union Prayerbook for the Days of Awe.* New York: CCAR, 1978, 1996.

Trible, Phyllis. *God and the Rhetoric of Sexuality.* Philadelphia: Fortress Press, 1978.

Walzer, Michael. *Exodus and Revolution.* New York: Basic Books, 1986.

Union Prayer Book. New York: CCAR, 1959.

Wright, Robert. *The Evolution of God.* New York: Little, Brown, 2009.